The Reading Race

The Reading Race

how every child can learn to read

Donna Awatere Huata

Huia

First published in 2002 by Huia Publishers
39 Pipitea St, PO Box 17-335
Welllington, Aotearoa New Zealand
www.huia.co.nz

ISBN: 1-877283-67-3

National Library of New Zealand Cataloguing-in-Publication Data
Huata, Donna Awatere.
The reading race : how every child can learn to read / Donna Awatere Huata.
Includes bibliographical references.
ISBN 1-877283-67-3
1. Reading – Phonetic method.
2. Language experience approach in education – New Zealand.
3. Literacy – New Zealand. I. Title.
372.4650993—dc 21

Dedication

To Wi Huata,
husband and father extraordinaire –
he tohu aroha ki a koe.

Acknowledgements

To my researcher, Berys Walters – many thanks;
To Professor Tom Nicholson, my editor who toned down my excessive language and who provided painstaking annotations – much gratitude;
To the Education and Science Select Committee of Brian Donnelly (NZ First); Gerry Brownlee and Maurice Williamson (National); Helen Duncan and Nanaia Mahuta (Labour) and our chair Dr Liz Gordon (Alliance), for agreeing to carry out the inquiry in the first place, for working long and hard hours over 18 months, for working together in a collegial and stimulating way to achieve 52 unanimous cross party recommendations setting out a blueprint for a reading nation – my deepest respect;
And to Scott Dennison, the best executive secretary any MP could hope for, keen rugby man, hard drinker and ex-apple picker from the Hawkes Bay – he mihi aroha ki a koe.

Contents

List of Abbreviations

ERO	Education Review Office
IEA	International Association for the Evaluation of Educational Achievement
NEMP	National Education Monitoring Project
NICHD	National Institute for Child Health and Development (United States)
NZEI	New Zealand Educational Institute
OECD	Organization for Economic Cooperation and Development
PISA	Programme for International Student Assessment
TIE	Targeted Individual Education

CHAPTER 1

The Problem — The Evidence

READING IS NOW AN ESSENTIAL SKILL TO FUNCTION AS A critical, thinking member of society. It's no accident that most prisoners can barely read. It's no accident that most unemployed people are barely literate. Reading is the single most important academic skill a person needs in modern life. Upon it we can predict how well someone will participate and succeed in society.

Over the last 30 years bureaucrats, politicians, academics, teacher trainers in the Ministry of Education and in tertiary institutions, and other vested interests have inflicted a tragedy on the youngest generations. Their educational experiment, sanctioned by successive governments, has failed thousands of our children.

In 2001 the failure of this experiment was exposed starkly when the Parliamentary Education and Science Select Committee reported on its Inquiry into Reading. In submissions to the Select Committee, numerous desperate parents wrote of their agony in trying to get help for their children who had failed to learn to read sufficiently well to keep up with their classmates. Frontline teachers and specialists, appalled by the ever increasing numbers of failed readers and never before able to report on these concerns to a select committee enquiry, agreed with them. It is time to stop the cover-up.

Reading failure gets worse as children reach adolescence. Many leave school for the dole queue, some getting involved in petty crime and perhaps serious crime. Studies have shown that 52 per cent of the prison population suffer a specific learning difficulty and a staggering 76 per cent have difficulty reading. Failure to teach children to read is in effect a 'dumbing down' of the whole population. Each individual case can cost the country hundreds of thousands of dollars – possibly millions. (In 1996 it cost $60,000 a year to keep a prisoner in a high-security jail and $30,000 a year to keep a child in care.[1])

The inability to read and write effectively diminishes human potential, learning potential, self-esteem, options and choices, the ability to think – make judgements, anticipate implications, think independently, to be adaptable and the ability to learn and grow throughout life. It leads to personal stress and frustration, family stress, community stress, employment difficulties, diminished workplace options, social difficulties and anti social behaviours.

Adrienne Nightingale, mother, classroom teacher, Reading Recovery trained teacher, and private tutor, describing her own experience in her submission to the Select Committee

A Christchurch mother's story, as she expressed it to the Education and Science Select Committee, was typical of many submissions from parents:[2]

> My bright and intelligent child was struggling to read at a very good and well-resourced primary school. He had a year of Reading Recovery in Year Two [six or seven years old] and still made little progress. During his Year Three I got so sick of hearing from the teachers – 'It's a boy thing, he'll get it soon'. At eight and a half he was still reading two years below his age level, yet was top of the class with Maths and with his verbal comprehension PAT score. He was near the bottom of the class with his written comprehension PAT. At last the school admitted something was wrong. On assessment by the Reading Recovery teacher he didn't even know his short vowels, was hopeless with his blends and had poor word attack skills. He is now having individual tuition from an SLD [students with learning disabilities] tutor from Seabrooke McKenzie Centre at the school. He is flourishing and starting to read independently after one year with **systematic letter sound** and **phonic tuition**. He is actually learning how words and sounds are made up, and can understand what he is trying to do and he is reading at last.

Why did her child fail to learn to read adequately? Her view is that:

> He was expected to pick up reading intuitively from context and practice. But he never got a grasp of the basics. He didn't have a clue what he was trying to do. He needed to be taught the tools, the rules, letter sounds, and phonics. As soon as he was taught this he started to read properly.

Many parents were bewildered by the resistance they encountered when they sought help outside the school. After one parent[3] contacted SPELD, for example, the teachers at her daughter's school:

> ... found this very threatening and tried to stop us getting this help ... . Eventually because of many struggles to get the school to understand and living in a small rural community as well as having to travel long distances to get SPELD help, at the age of 10 we sent her to boarding school. To date her education has cost us $55,000. She is now in the sixth form.

For this parent, the cause of the failure was that the school was limited to a whole language approach and did not cater for children who struggled to learn in this way. She felt there was a lack of understanding of learning disabilities and the problems faced by children with them.

Each of these determined parents who wrote to the Select Committee eventually broke through the system's blinkered approach and found the help she needed for her child. Yet those who promote the system applaud New Zealand as a world leader in reading instruction. So how can there be anything wrong with it?

Breaking through the barriers

Julie Tate expresses her despair in her submission to the Education and Science Select Committee:

> *My son was at school for two years, not reading, not even learning the alphabet, or the sounds the letters made ... I used to do parent help each week in the reading class so the teacher could spend more time with [him]. But she couldn't help him with his special learning needs and the programme he required ... . This child was slowly becoming frustrated and falling behind his peers. The frustration finally led to him blowing his stack and being suspended indefinitely from school. He had to shift towns to get a school that wanted to help him. We did find that school after trying many.*

Although this boy had several deep-seated learning disabilities, after just two months of individual tuition for two hours each week, his class teacher reported improvement:

> *He is virtually ready to break through the barrier in sound to letter correspondence even though he still finds reading a frustrating subject.*

His mother reported that the boy now looked forward to going to school. His attitude had changed fundamentally from anger about failing in his learning to laughter and happiness about school. He was picking up books at home and endeavouring to read them. This almost miraculous change had been achieved because he had received help in working on a range of physical and perceptual weaknesses combined with texts for listening skills, decoding skills and writing practice.

Many involved with the system have had reason to question it. As a Wellington teacher[4] wrote to the Select Committee:

> In over twenty years of working with parents, schools have been seen as a place where for many they have failed ... . The system and methods used to teach children to read through the introduction of whole language leading to Reading Recovery programmes has had disastrous effects and consequences for many generations of children, adults and society. Furthermore illiteracy has become epidemic in this country which has led to an underclass and continuing cycle of generations of failure for many regardless of race, creed or intelligence.

Are New Zealanders therefore becoming less literate? The answer is hard to uncover because in the past New Zealand had few objective measures of national literacy standards, such as national assessment measures.[5] In the mid 1980s, from an analysis of previous survey data Professor Graham Nuthall[6] concluded that standards of spelling had fallen consistently since the 1930s. While acknowledging that his findings were tentative because of the lack of national survey data, he observed that:

> It is easy for officials to dismiss complaints about the lowering of standards in schools as just another aspect of the way the older generation fails to understand and appreciate the young ... . However, a modern public school system costs a lot of money ... and it should be the responsibility of the government to ensure that this money is well spent.

Even as late as 1994, lack of national assessment data remained a problem. Neil Reid of the New Zealand Council for Educational Research complained that New Zealand still had no national system to monitor student achievement. In basic skill areas such as reading, writing and mathematics the evidence was fragmentary, especially between 1981 and 1990.[7] It took an international survey[8] in 1990 to reveal that New Zealand was no longer leading the world in literacy – in contrast to its performance in a similar survey conducted 20 years earlier.

In 1985 New Zealand was regarded as one of the most literate countries on earth. Reading educators beat a path to our schools to find out about the whole language approach to literacy instruction. By the end of the century, in comparison to other countries, our level of reading achievement had fallen. Today despite a new English curriculum and resource materials, despite the reforms of Tomorrow's Schools and despite the investment in Reading Recovery, the reading achievement of nine and 14 year olds has fallen, relative to other countries. Of particular concern is the achievement of Maori and Pacific Islanders and the reading comprehension of many 14 year olds.

David Whitehead, University of Waikato School of Education, submission to the Select Committee

The evidence, 1970–2000

According to National Reading Recovery data covering the years up until the mid 1990s, as many as 25 per cent (one in four) of our six-year-olds received remedial reading assistance.[9] Since the mid 1990s the method of calculating the numbers in Reading Recovery has changed to give a more conservative estimate. Yet even the adjusted figures showed 20 per cent of six-year-olds were in this programme in 1995. By far the largest proportion of children enrolled are Maori and Pacific Islands children, especially boys.

By 2000 the proportion of children in the programme had declined to 20 per cent using the traditional estimate or 16 per cent using the conservative estimate.[10] Several factors, however, indicate that 20 per cent is likely to be an underestimate of children requiring remedial reading in 2000. First, the programme is now available to fewer children. In 2000 about 100 fewer schools were offering Reading Recovery (available in 82 per cent of all schools) than in 1995 (when it was available in 90 per cent of all schools). Second, many children who need Reading Recovery may not be getting that help. For example, only 47 per cent of children on the East Coast have access to Reading Recovery, compared to 82 per cent in the south of the North Island, and the programme reaches only 50 per cent of rural schools. Moreover, each school has a set percentage of children they can accept for Reading Recovery, meaning they may have to exclude many children who need help.

It is of concern that the only major intervention available to six-year-olds in New Zealand is becoming less accessible. Even more worrying is that, as demonstrated by research on the effectiveness of Reading Recovery during the 1990s, many of the six-year-old children in the programme derived little long-term benefit from it. This disastrous performance was an issue that troubled the Education and Science Select Committee. Children who need early intervention deserve a better outcome.

Introduced to monitor reading standards, the first National Education Monitoring Project (NEMP) collected data on reading in 1995. It used a 'light sampling' approach, assessing only a small proportion of children in the country, and set reading tasks that 100 per cent of children should be able to do at a given age. As reported in the media in 1997,[11] the results showed that approximately 20 per cent of 8- and 12-year-olds were reading below levels regarded as acceptable for their age level.

From a different perspective, further evidence of New Zealand's poor performance in reading came from a 1997 International Adult Literacy Survey.[12] It found that nearly half our adults were reading 'below the minimum level of competence'. In addition, a fifth had very poor skills – a finding consistent with data from Reading Recovery and from the NEMP survey.

In total then, the evidence indicates that at least a fifth of New Zealand children are very poor readers. Yet, according to the journal of the American Federation of Teachers,[13] this number could be much smaller – indeed 19 out of 20 children can be taught to read and spell competently **if properly taught**. We can reduce our present failure rate from 4 in 20 to 1 in 20. Conversely, if we do nothing to change the present system, then 3 in 20 of our children will continue to lose out.

The most widely quoted data on the extent of the problem are provided by the cross-national surveys of the International Association for the Evaluation of Educational Achievement (IEA). IEA members, who are educators from more than 50 countries, meet annually to plan surveys of the

In the mid 1980s it was concluded from an analysis of previous survey data that standards of spelling had fallen consistently since the 1930s.

Alexander Turnbull Library, Wellington F23725¼

teaching and learning of students in their national schools. From this basis, the reading comprehension of New Zealand 14-year-olds was surveyed in 1970 and again in 1990.[14] Although it is difficult to compare the results directly as the two surveys used different criteria, one disturbing trend is clear: New Zealand's ethnic, socioeconomic and gender gaps in reading comprehension are widening. From being relatively small in 1970, by 1990 the gaps were greater than those in any other country surveyed.

In the 1970 survey, New Zealand 14-year-olds had the highest average reading score for their age group out of 15 countries, including England, Scotland, the United States and Finland.[15] In 1990 they were fourth out of the 32 countries in the survey, still ahead of the United States but behind Finland, France and Sweden (England and Scotland did not participate in the 1990 survey).[16] The 1990 survey also assessed other age groups. It showed other countries were ahead of New Zealand at the 10-year-old level. Our nine-year-olds came sixth, behind Finland (first) and the United States (second) – countries that New Zealand had surpassed in 1970.

Even more significant than the drop in our ranking is the range of variation in the scores. As Tom Nicholson points out, if a country with a high average mean score also has a lot of people scoring very low or very high, the higher scores of the best readers are propping up the lower scores of the poorest readers.[17] In 1970 New Zealand's spread of scores around the average score (called the standard deviation) was similar to that of other countries. For all 15 countries the standard deviation was on average 10.6; New Zealand's standard deviation was 11.0. In 1990, by contrast, we had a wider range than any other country in the survey. The average standard deviation for member countries of the Organization for Economic Cooperation and Development (OECD) was 74.5; ours was 92. More New Zealand children were at the extreme ends of the achievement range. We were top heavy and bottom heavy.

To summarise, there was no large gap in reading achievement among New Zealand children in 1970. Our spread of scores was close to the international average. New Zealand outperformed other countries in reading because there was a high overall level of reading achievement. By 1990 New Zealand had the widest reading gap in the OECD. The situation had become worse for the poorest readers and better for the best readers. A 1998 OECD follow-up analysis[18] of these results, which compared the 1990 top quarter of students with the bottom quarter, confirmed that New Zealand had the greatest gap between the top 25 per cent and bottom 25 per cent of readers.

Tragically for New Zealand children, the education clique are determined to sell the survey results as a positive endorsement of their reading programmes. They are taking credit for the top achievers as beneficiaries of the 'whole language' reading approach used in schools. They are also finding reasons other than the reading approach to explain the poorer achievement of the bottom 25 per cent. Here's how John Smith and Warwick Elley[19] interpreted the results:

> New Zealand actually had more students in the top quarter internationally than any other country. ... The outstanding abilities of our top quarter were offset by a substantial group of weaker students – students who frequently come from poor and bookless homes, who spoke another language at home, who spent more hours watching TV than they spent at school, and who were more often of Maori or Pacific Island origin.

However, the importance of the standard deviations cannot be ignored. If the variance is small, as in the 1970 survey, it means that the teaching system is delivering a reasonable quality of instruction to all children. It is possible to achieve this same quality nationwide because New Zealand has a national system of education. The same primers, beginner reading books and journals are freely available to all schools. Teachers receive a compulsory level of training over a compulsory time period. That was the system in 1970 and it remained the same until 1990. The only major change over the intervening 20 years was the introduction of a new way of teaching reading, called the whole language approach.[20] Its introduction was backed up by a new set of graded reading books in the late 1970s and early 1980s. There was also a national inservice training programme for all teachers in the whole language method of teaching. The new approach was introduced without conducting any research to compare its merits with the previous approach, and without establishing any system of ongoing monitoring. The outcome of the whole language approach was not clear until the results of the 1990 IEA survey were publicised.

From the available national and international data in the early to mid 1990s, then, there was evidence to suggest that reading standards had fallen. It seemed that 20 per cent of children were not reading successfully, as reflected in Reading Recovery data and 1995 NEMP results. The fall in reading standards was felt particularly by children in low-income groups, especially Maori and Pacific Islands pupils. The old rhetoric that New Zealand had the best readers in the world no longer convinced the general public.

In 1998 the then National–New Zealand First coalition government introduced a Reading by Nine initiative, with funding for new programmes to help failing readers, and a Literacy Taskforce of experts and laypeople to investigate the issues. The government also adopted the goal that: 'By 2005 every child turning nine will be able to read, write and do maths for success.'

The Reading by Nine initiative was prompted by the negative results for Maori and Pacific Islands children. All the data on Maori reading achievement indicated significant problems, especially for Maori from low-income backgrounds. The Education Review Office (ERO) reported in 1996 that schools

New Zealand studies show that children who fall behind in reading at age five are likely to be still behind at age nine. These findings contradict the notion that children will begin to learn to read when they are 'ready'.

Ans Westra, 1963. Alexander Turnbull Library, Wellington M309

with high proportions of Maori and Pacific Islands children had very high percentages of children failing to read.[21] This claim was supported by data from a 1995 University of Auckland survey of 13-year-old high school students in some of Auckland's poorest suburbs, which showed that nearly 9 out of 10 students in the survey were reading below the national average.[22] A breakdown by ethnicity showed that the worst readers were Pacific Islands and Asian students in schools located in low-income areas. However, the results could not be explained as solely due to cultural factors or speaking a language other than English at home, because Pakeha (European) and Maori students in poor areas, though below the national average, were reading at about the same levels.

The reading gap between rich and poor

Who are the bottom 20 per cent of readers? They are the ones who are blamed for being from poor, bookless homes where they watch too much TV. Teachers often reassure those parents who dare to speak out that their children will eventually catch up. But the teachers themselves are also often victims. In the face of such inexplicable failure of the system that they have religiously followed, they have not received from **their** educators the skills and knowledge required to diagnose the reasons for the failure and to remedy it.

The truth is that children don't catch up. It becomes much harder to improve reading, spelling and writing skills after about the age of nine. Longitudinal studies in New Zealand have shown that children who fall behind in reading at age five are likely to be behind still at age nine. These findings contradict the notion that children will begin to learn to read when they are 'ready'.

In 2000 Tom Nicholson and other researchers in the School of Education at The University of Auckland reported the results of a five-year study of the reading progress of children attending school in high- and low-income areas. The children were assessed several times from school entry at five years of age through until they were nearly 10 years old.[23] Among the children in high-income areas, by age seven reading accuracy and comprehension levels were a year ahead of chronological age. By age 10, on average, reading accuracy was still a year ahead and reading comprehension was six months ahead. In contrast, by age seven children from low-income areas, who were predominantly Maori and Pacific Islanders, had reading accuracy and comprehension levels that were six months behind chronological age. By age 10 reading accuracy was seven months behind chronological age and reading comprehension was 18 months behind.

In comparing the relative progress of children from rich and poor schools over the first few years of primary education, Nicholson and colleagues found that the reading gap widened markedly by seven years of age and grew wider after that. At age seven the gap between schools in low- and high-socio-economic areas was 1.2 years in accuracy and 1.3 years in comprehension. When the children were nearly 10 years old this gap had increased to 1.9 years in accuracy and 2.0 years in comprehension. Unfortunately, the children who are predominantly in schools in the poorest areas of Auckland are Maori and Pacific Islanders, while those in the most affluent areas are Pakeha.

This trend was highlighted in the 1990 IEA survey. As the 1998 report of the government's own Literacy Taskforce acknowledged, the evidence from the survey suggests that there are:[24]

> ... initial disparities that then continue to grow over the first four years of schooling between Maori and Pacific Islands children on the one hand and the Pakeha children on the other, as well as disparities between children in low-decile schools and those in other schools. It was noted that there is a high proportion of Maori and Pacific Islands children in low-decile schools.
>
> Analyses of school leaver qualifications data and the Adult Literacy Survey show lower levels of performance for Maori and Pacific Island people than for Pakeha, which suggests that later learning has not redressed these problems. This clearly has further implications for generational effects on children's literacy learning.

Although the lack of good quality information about student achievement in literacy had restricted the efficacy of its findings, as it stated to the Education and Science Select Committee, the ERO too found low achievement in many schools in Otara and Mangere, the East Coast and the far north. At the top of its list of obstructions to effective teaching of reading was lack of teacher knowledge and skills.

The shocking fact is that literacy problems are discriminatory. They are far more prevalent among boys, the poor and non-Pakeha. Perhaps these gaps do arise from gender, economic and cultural differences as claimed by the educrats and their acolytes. But so what? We know they are not inevitable. Research shows that literacy gaps persist where schools fail to provide effective instruction. Once a gap opens up, it is likely to widen as children move on through the grades. On the other hand, where high quality instruction is offered, the gaps diminish. The first two years are crucial in tackling the problem. Surely so-called professional experts should get over their blaming and finger pointing and get on with the vital job of closing that gap. The solutions are out there.

For example, in his submission to the Education and Science Select Committee, Tom Nicholson recommended a three-pronged strategy:

1. As New Zealand research has shown that the inclusion of phonemic awareness and phonological recoding skills in the present classroom setting gets children off to a better start, the government needs to commission the development of structured reading resources by independent agencies with research and specialist expertise in how to teach phonological recoding skills, phonemic awareness and alphabet knowledge.

2. An independent research institution should be commissioned to track 'at risk' children. It should produce annual reports on the state of their literacy, which will enable the government to assess whether teaching reforms are effective.

3. The knowledge base of teachers needs to be increased so they can provide more effective instruction and can use a range of different teaching approaches. The government should designate preferred training providers with international reputations to implement specialist degrees for teachers of reading.

Latest evidence, 2001

A few weeks prior to the publication of the Education and Science Select Committee report, a new report from the National Education Monitoring Project was released.[25] From a survey of 3,000 children aged 8 and 12 years in 260 schools in the year 2000, the NEMP had found reading standards had improved considerably since its survey in 1995. Among 8-year-olds, the proportion who were reading at above average levels had increased from 32 to 48 per cent, while the proportion at below average levels had dropped from 20 to 12 per cent. Changes were smaller among 12-year-olds: above average levels increased from 50 to 56 per cent, while below average levels dropped slightly from 20 to 19 per cent.

These findings seem to indicate that reading standards improved between 1995 and 2000, especially at the 8-year-old level. The reasons were not clear and the NEMP did not speculate on them; its report stated, 'It is not the role of NEMP to pass judgement and enter debate.' However, high proportions of children – 12 per cent of 8-year-olds and 19 per cent of 12-year-olds – were still not succeeding, and there remained significant gaps in reading among Maori, Pacific Islands and Pakeha children.

Also in 2001 the government announced the results of a new survey, called the Programme for International Student Assessment (PISA),[26] which compared the literacy levels of a quarter of a million

15- and 16-year-olds in 32 OECD countries, including Brazil, Russia, Japan, Mexico, the United Kingdom, Australia and New Zealand. In terms of average levels of literacy achievement, Finland and Canada were placed at the top and New Zealand came third. However, New Zealand still had 14 per cent of students reading at the lowest levels of the survey and 19 per cent at the highest levels, representing a higher proportion of the best readers than any other country. Consider the size of this gap in comparison with the findings for other countries:

	Readers at the lowest level	**Readers at the highest level**
New Zealand	14 per cent	19 per cent
Finland	7 per cent	18 per cent
Korea	6 per cent	6 per cent
Canada	9 per cent	17 per cent
Japan	10 per cent	10 per cent
Ireland	11 per cent	14 per cent.

As the above figures indicate, although Korea was placed sixth in the survey, in overall terms it had more to boast than the 'top three' countries. Korea as a whole scored above the average for the 32 OECD countries. More importantly, it had more students in the middle levels, 89 per cent between the top band and the bottom band of achievement. When you include the very top band, 94 per cent of Korean students scored above the lowest level; in contrast, only 86 per cent of New Zealand students scored above the lowest level. If a country is really committed to serving its children well, it will deliver high levels of literacy to as many children as possible. Korea has done this better than anyone else.

Conclusions

How children feel about themselves as readers and how they behave in class depend on their success in learning to read and the difficulty level of their reading material. Children who do not read well feel bad about themselves as readers and are likely to resist the academic tasks of the classroom. Twenty years ago when I developed my Otara Reading Programme, I worked from the principle of giving children materials that they could 'comfortably' read and put into practice a reading toolkit based on phonics. I hypothesised that with early success the children were more likely to become competent readers, feel good about themselves and behave well in class. My conjecture proved to be correct. The result is not unique. SPELD teachers and others who have jettisoned whole language dogma have reported consistently that other methods work more effectively in the interests of their students.

Faced with the growing evidence of thousands of young people failed by this system and the damage that a failure to read inflicts on many young lives, how can those responsible for schools avoid examining the whole language approach used in schools when it has been questioned by many researchers and rejected by governments in other countries such as the United Kingdom and the United States? How can they dare to explain away the successes achieved through alternative teaching methods? How can they blame literacy failures on children themselves, their socioeconomic situation, poor diet or the lack of English spoken in their homes? How can those in charge of schools not look to themselves and to their teaching methods?

The reason there is no outcry about the ERO report that reading failure is as high as 60 per cent in some South Auckland primary schools is that there is an unspoken assumption that children from poorer homes, benefit-dependent homes, and Maori and Pacific Islands homes cannot be expected to read at the normal rates. Principals, teachers, colleges of education and the Ministry of Education conspire to shrug off widespread reading failure. Most children of opinion makers, public servants and teachers learn to read without any problem. Why then should these people concern themselves about children who don't learn to read? The way reading is taught generally suits their children, so why all the fuss?

According to the dominant brand of radical educational theory in New Zealand, the main reasons for low educational achievement lie in social injustice and inequality. As Geoffrey Partington[27] points out, this attitude readily leads schools to:

> ... neglect the immediate tasks they ought much more to attend to, and in which they might well succeed, in favour of rhetorical attacks on social conditions external to the schools and not directly amenable to their influence.

In addition, it is difficult to change a mindset that has existed for decades against phonics. There is a reluctance to accept that the experiment of whole language teaching, with its accompanying rejection of phonics, was a mistake. As Massey University historian Roger Openshaw[28] has written, 'The historical method of teaching reading through emphasis on phonics and grammar became in effect a dirty word among teachers.'

The moral duty of any public education system should be to make all children achieve the highest level of literacy that is possible. But the evidence is that the New Zealand system is not delivering this result. Those responsible for schools put the onus on early childhood services to solve the reading problems in schools. The emphasis nowadays is on the importance of a child's preschool experiences as preparation for reading. But this shifts responsibility from professional educators to untrained parents and caregivers, in a way that disadvantages children from poor, uneducated and non-European households. The children in these households are the ones who depend most on the public school system to help them break out of their cycle of disadvantage. While parent input is beneficial, the prime responsibility for literacy instruction must remain with those who are paid to teach our children well – the schools, the curriculum developers and the colleges of education – and they need to get over their prejudices and do a much better job of teaching our children to read.

Notes

1 Awatere-Huata, D. (1996). *My Journey*. Seaview Press.

2 Dawson, Sarah. (2000). Submission to the Education and Science Select Committee, 342W.

3 Daly, Faye. (2000). Submission to the Education and Science Select Committee, 129W.

4 Bennett, June Frances. (2000). Submission to the Education and Science Select Committee, 39.

5 Taylor, Rowan. (2000). Submission to the Education and Science Select Committee, 352.

6 Nuthall, G. (1985). Standards of achievement in schools. *Economic Bulletin*, No. 702, 1–5; p.1.

7 Reid, N. (1994). How literate are kiwis? Who knows (or cares)? *Reading Forum NZ*, No. 2, 3–24.

8 Elley, W.B. (1992). *How in the world do students read?* Hamburg, Germany: International Association for the Evaluation of Educational Achievement.
See also: Wagemaker, H. (1993). Reading achievement of New Zealand 9- and 14-year-olds. In H. Wagemaker (Ed.), *Achievement in reading literacy. New Zealand's performance in a national and international context.* Wellington: Ministry of Education.

9 Kerslake, J. (1996). A summary of the 1995 data on Reading Recovery. *Research Bulletin*, 7, 23–27.

10 Kerslake, J. (2001). Annual monitoring of Reading Recovery: the data for 2000. *Research Bulletin*, 12, 65–71.

11 Crooks, T., & Flockton, L. (1997). *National Education Monitoring Project forum newssheet*. Dunedin: Otago University Educational Assessment Research Unit.

12 Ministry of Education. (1997). *Adult literacy in New Zealand: Results from the international adult literacy survey (1996)*. Wellington: Author.

13 American Federation of Teachers. (1995) *American Educator*

14 Elley (1992) – see note 8.

15 Thorndike, R.L. (1973). *Reading comprehension in 15 countries*. New York: John Wiley.

16 Elley (1992) – see note 8.

17 Nicholson, Tom. (2000). Submission to the Education and Science Select Committee, 357.

18 Organization for Economic Cooperation and Development. (1998). *Overcoming failure at school*. Paris: Author.

19 Smith, J.W., & Elley, W.B. (1994). *How children learn to read in New Zealand*. Auckland: Longman; p. 113.

20 Nicholson, T. (2000). *Reading the writing on the wall: Debates, challenges and opportunities in the teaching of reading*. Palmerston North: Dunmore Press.

21 Education Review Office. (1996). *Improving Schooling in Mangere and Otara*. Wellington: Author.

22 Nicholson, T., & Gallienne, G. (1995). A survey of reading achievement levels among 13-year-old pupils in two contrasting socio-economic areas. *New Zealand Journal of Educational Studies*, *30*, 115–123.

23 Nicholson, T., McIntosh, S., & Grant, F. (2000, July). *What makes for a better start in literacy? The results of a five- year study*. Paper presented at Ministry of Education Pre-World Congress Seminar, Auckland.

24 Ministry of Education. (1998). *Report of the Literacy Taskforce*. Wellington: Author.

25 Flockton, L., & Crooks, T. (2001). *Reading and speaking: assessment results 2000*. National Education Monitoring Project Report. Dunedin: Education Assessment Research Unit for the Ministry of Education.

26 Organization of Economic Cooperation and Development. (2001). *Knowledge and skills for life: First results from PISA 2000*. Paris: Author.

27 Partington, G. (1998). *Teacher education and training in New Zealand*. Wellington: New Zealand Education Forum; p. 92.

28 Openshaw, R. (Ed.) (1991). *Schooling in the '40s and '50s: An oral history*. Palmerston North: Massey University, Educational Research and Developmental Centre; p. 70.

CHAPTER 2

How Did We Get Here?

CHILDREN UP TO THE AGE OF FIVE ACCUMULATE A VOCABULARY of anything up to 10,000 words through some sort of inbuilt instinct for language.[1] The trick then is for them to find out what these vocalised words look like in printed form. In all English-speaking countries we use an alphabet of 26 letters and up to 44 sounds (called phonemes). This is the focus of reading – what these sounds look like on paper.

1877 and all that ... the ABC method

In New Zealand after 1877, when school first became compulsory, reading was still being taught by the ABC method.[2] Everyone started by learning the names of the letters of the alphabet. They learned the alphabet forwards and backwards until they knew the names of all the letters. Then they learned to read two-letter syllables, like *ab*, *eb*, *ib*, *ob*, *ub*. They moved on to three-letter syllables and then to word-building activities.

From Hugh Price's review of inspectors' reports between 1877 and 1900, it appears that inspectors at the time thought the ABC method was difficult for many children, as much of the instruction involved rote drill and practice.[3] In New Zealand schools after 1877, learning to read was made even more difficult because there were often not enough copies of the school reader to go around the class. Because children could not progress to the next class until they could read their current reader, rote memorisation was emphasised. Here is an example of an illustrated passage of two-letter words from an early primer, *The Royal Crown Primer*, published in 1872:[4]

> I am up on an ox. It is to go in, so am I. No, my ox is to go on. Am I by my ox? No I am on it; so I am. Is my ox to go in? Yes it is to go in. Go in my ox; go in.

6 ROYAL PRIMER.

a at

c	a	t
r	a	t
m	a	t

cat. rat. mat.

ROYAL PRIMER. 7

a · at · cat.

1.
A cat. A rat.
On a mat.

2.
A fat cat sat on the mat.

3.
Is it a hat? It is my hat.

The *New Royal Primer*, published in 1885, reflects the ABC approach to reading instruction. After learning the names of all the letters of the alphabet, children learned to read two-letter then three letter syllables, and then moved to word-building activities.

Alexander Turnbull Library, Wellington B-K 547-667

Between 1877 and 1900 inspectors complained about the way children were made to memorise their text material for the purpose of appearing to be good readers. Children chanted their lessons mindlessly in unison. They learned words by spelling them according to their letter names, as in *tee, haitch, ee* spells *the*. It was really a spelling method. Another problem was that the names of the letters did not give the child a way of 'sounding out' the word. The ABC method endured because the names of the letters in the alphabet seemed the obvious place to begin and for all its faults many children were able to learn with this approach.

By the early 1900s schools were making use of several approaches to teaching reading. It was recommended that teachers use a range of approaches, including the whole word approach, the sentence method and phonics.

It's hard to pinpoint exactly when the ABC method went out of fashion. The process was probably a gradual one. For example, writing about her experiences in schools from 1919 to 1949 in a teacher magazine published by the Department (now Ministry) of Education, a teacher mentioned that in her first year as a teacher in 1919 her classroom still had a reading chart that read, 'Is it an ox? It is an ox.' But the ABC method was gradually being replaced by competing reading series. And by 1929 the ABC method was definitely 'out'. In that year the Department of Education produced a new syllabus in which it was clear that the days of reading 'I am up on an ox' were over. For example, Beacon readers, adapted in England from the United States, were used in schools in the 1920s. They had appealing stories like *Chicken Licken* and *Three Billy Goats Gruff*. In the Beacon series, phonics teaching was delayed for at least the first school term. There was also a 'look and say' series used in schools in the 1920s called *Live Readers*, written by Miss Dorothy Baster and published locally by Whitcombe and Tombs.

The rise of phonics 1930–1950 ... *Progressive Readers*

In 1928 a new locally produced phonics series called *Progressive Readers* was published by Whitcombe and Tombs. Commonly used in schools until 1950, they were by far the most popular reading series.[5] They were graded to match the child's growing phonics knowledge, starting very simply with almost all regular words and just a few irregular words and getting progressively richer in vocabulary as the child's reading knowledge grew. The accompanying manual recommended quick visualisation of words as 'sight words' in the initial stages until 30 words were learned and then the teacher was to introduce phonics.

Here is an example of the use of phonically regular words in a *Progressive Reader*:

> 'Grunt, grunt,' said Little Black Pig. 'I do not wish to stay in my sty. I do not wish to lie in the mud. I wish to fly. I think I can fly up to the sky. I shall try.'

The rise of look and say 1950—1960 ... *Janet and John*

By the end of the 1940s the *Progressive Readers* had been used non-stop, with few modifications, for more than 20 years. It appears that by this time the *Progressive Readers* were no longer popular. In 1951 the Ministry of Education introduced the *Janet and John* series. It was printed in New Zealand under licence from the London publishing company Nisbet and issued to all New Zealand schools. The series was adapted from an American series called *Jerry and Alice*.

Although *Janet and John* included some phonics, the series was concerned primarily with encouraging children to read words by using meaning cues and their overall 'look'. For example, teachers were to teach children to recognise new words in each little primer by writing the words on cards, showing the cards to the children briefly and asking the children to read each one quickly. Another technique was to write new words on the blackboard as single words and practise reading them with the children before reading them in a new story. The idea was to put the new words into memory as visual wholes, so it was important to practise reading the words individually in lists of words to be learned as sight words.

Janet and John books were colourful and up-to-date, and became a staple diet for beginning readers in England, Australia and New Zealand. These are the stories that 1950s pupils remember from their school days. The stories revolved around a two-parent, two-child family and their dog. For example (from *Here we go*):

> Little dog. Come little dog. Come. Come and look. Janet, Janet. Come and look. See the little dog.

Looking back, can we claim that look and say was a better way of learning to read than phonics? Many children learned to read with *Janet and John*, but there were problems with the look and say approach. Rudolf Flesch criticised it strongly in *Why Johnny can't read*, published in 1955 in the United States.[6] He argued that phonics gives a way of figuring out new words by connecting print with spoken language. Phonics alerts the child to the principle that the printed word is just the spoken word written down. On the other hand the whole word system, as presented in standard graded readers, sacrificed

The locally produced *Progressive Readers* formed the most popular reading series for about two decades from the 1930s. Based on a phonics approach to reading instruction, they were graded to match the child's growing phonics knowledge.

Alexander Turnbull Library, Wellington B-K 545-COVER

these benefits in order to give children a cheap way of recognising the shapes of familiar words instantly. The cheap way was to learn new words as sight words.[7]

So, although the child might appear to be reading, it was really a kind of rote learning that would eventually come unstuck. For example, a child might recognise *dog* because of the 'tail' on the end of the *g*, but what happens with *frog*, where there is also a tail on the *g*? Many children found that sheer memorisation of words according to their look could not be sustained, as too many words started to look the same. The reason why many children managed to learn to read under this system is that they mentally discarded the holistic strategy at a certain point and started to analyse words according to their letter sounds. The problem was that the look and say approach did not necessarily lead children to make inferences about letters and sounds in this way. Therefore many children stuck with the visual learning that the approach encouraged, relying on distinctive cues, such as the tail on *dog*, and on context cues to guess at words. As a result, their reading progress fell behind. This was the criticism that critics such as Rudolf Flesch levelled at the *Janet and John* books: that although children could learn to read that way, many would not.

The beginnings of whole language 1960—1970 ... *Ready to Read*

By the end of the 1950s the New Zealand government decided to drop the *Janet and John* series. Stocks of the books were low and at the time the country was short of foreign funds. The government asked if it would be possible to produce a home-grown series to replace *Janet and John*, and the Department of Education agreed to do this. *Janet and John* had not done anything wrong from their point of view. They were replaced for financial reasons.

In many ways the new series, introduced in the 1960s, was similar to *Janet and John*. It used graded vocabulary, with each new book just a little bit harder than the previous book. It also used the 'little books' concept that had been part of Janet and John approach to teaching beginners. The series, called *Ready to Read*, was produced under the direction of an inspector of schools, Myrtle Simpson.

Although the new books seemed similar to *Janet and John*, they were very different in theory. It was not just that the *Ready to Read* books were about New Zealand children and stories. Myrtle Simpson also introduced a new way of teaching, which later turned out to be very similar to the philosophy of whole language. It was argued that the *Janet and John* books had not used enough natural language, which made it difficult for children to read for meaning. It was argued that if the stories were well written, using natural language, children could learn new words while they were reading, rather than having to read them beforehand as lists.

This idea that children could learn to read by using context and picture cues in the story to identify new words, took New Zealand down a new pathway in terms of reading method, which led toward what is now called the whole language approach. As Professor Tom Nicholson noted about *Ready to Read* in 1997:[8]

> What was really remarkable about the series was that it was uninfluenced by the 1950s debate about phonics especially in the United States that had been stirred up by the publication of *Why Johnny can't read*. ... Yet thousands of miles away in New Zealand, the 1962 *Ready to Read* series seemed just like the look-say material Flesch had denounced.

Despite appearances, however, *Ready to Read* had gone a step further than *Janet and John*. It embraced a new set of ideas about reading that had not been researched before. A new researcher, Marie Clay, made this new series the subject of her PhD thesis. She studied the reading progress of 100 children in their first year of school who were taught with the new series of books. The results from Clay's point of view showed that children could learn to read this way, even though they did not receive explicit instruction in phonics. As she put it:[9]

> There are other ways of learning to read with the primary emphasis on sounds, letters or sight words, but the description of reading behaviour which emerged in this research seems to approximate closely what the mature reader does.

At this time, too, similar ideas about learning to read by immersing children in the reading of stories were emanating from the United States and Canada. The way children were learning to read in New Zealand was soon called the psycholinguistic approach. What Myrtle Simpson had done in the development of *Ready to Read* was to show how the psycholinguistic approach could be put into practice.

Ready to Read aimed to use more 'natural language' than the old *Janet and John* books had. In the new readers, children went to New Zealand schools, lived in New Zealand homes and took their pet lambs and calves to pet shows. The first little books were titled *Early in the morning*, *Grandma comes to stay* and *The fire engine*. The teaching methods were in line with the principles of the whole language approach. The new handbook for the *Ready to Read* series emphasised the importance of teaching reading in the context of reading stories, rather than teaching lists of words in isolation. Using flash cards and teaching words out of the context of a story were discouraged. It was argued that these activities stopped children from doing their own learning. The teacher started

From what I remember, Myrtle Simpson got the idea that if children learned to read using their natural language, through the experience of reading, and talking through a story with an adult, probably a teacher or mature reader, that they could actually learn in that way. Rather than having to be taught the words and taught phonics, they developed a reading system for themselves.

Shirley Nalder, reflecting on her teaching experiences[10]

The Ready to Read *theorists rightly insisted on the abolition of all the grinding blackboard pre-teaching and practice; from the moment that* Ready to Read *came in, words were meant to be deciphered in the books, in context, bringing insights that would lead to more independence, more skill with word analysis and greater joy.*

Beverley Randell, **Shaping the PM Story Books**

There were difficulties at first. The subject matter was middle class, not suited to Maori or Polynesian children. I can remember thinking of one book, Grandma Comes to Stay, *and here is Grandma landing in an aeroplane to stay with her relations and father going to meet her in the car after having shaved himself with an electric razor. People thought, 'Well, what on earth did that have to do with the Maori child down in the Urewera country?'*

Ruth Evans[11]

with a book (rather than blackboard pre-teaching as with *Janet and John*) and read it to the class, encouraging the children to make letter–sound rules by making analogies to known words. Children were to learn to read through reading.

This approach was called 'the method of teaching from the books as the need arose'. Phonetic analysis occurred only when the teacher felt the children were ready for it and only when the text material provided an opportunity to illustrate a phonic principle. It was phonics 'as the need arose'. The new approach represented a definite move away from direct teaching of phonics, as well as a move away from look and say, especially the idea of children learning sight words. Instead, the assumption built into *Ready to Read* books was that children would unconsciously work out for themselves the letter–sound rules.

In the handbook she prepared for teachers, Myrtle Simpson described how to teach small groups of children by reading aloud the *Ready to Read* little books and how to use context, picture cues and sometimes letter cues to figure out words the children could not recognise. There was no 'sounding out' of complete words. The children would look at the first couple of letters (like *sh* in *shaving*) or a meaningful part of a word (like *day* in *today*). If they learned letter–sound rules at all, they did so implicitly.

The *Ready to Read* books were graded but introduced new words at a steeper rate than the *Janet and John* readers had; the rate was now one new word in 10 running words instead of one in 20. It was soon recognised that the word rate was too difficult and would lead to 'frustration level' reading. The new readers would need to be reinforced by supporting books such as the *PM Story Books*.[12]

Putting whole language in place 1970s ... winning hearts and minds

During the 1970s the Department of Education also made available considerable resources to provide inservice courses for teachers. The Early Reading Inservice Course (ERIC) was offered to thousands of teachers around the country. Later, teachers of older primary children had the opportunity to take the Later Reading Inservice Course (LARIC). Both inservice courses were full of whole language ideas about learning and teaching reading. A radio series for parents in 1978 explained that children learned to read by reading and that they did not need to sound out words. Canadian writer Frank Smith's ideas on predicting meaning in reading also underpinned the new wisdom, as did his comment, 'It is only through reading that children learn to read'. Reading had become 'contextualised'.[13]

How had New Zealand's education policy developed in this way? A number of opinion leaders in the curriculum division of the Department of Education and in the advisory service had jumped on to the whole language bandwagon. They genuinely felt that the new psycholinguistic approach was right for New Zealand. Psycholinguistic theory rejected phonics as a reductionist approach to reading, which started with the sounds of letters rather than with the book itself. Such views influenced the political decision-makers to the exclusion of other perspectives. And to be fair, the psycholinguistic viewpoint generated huge support in the 1970s and 1980s, not just in New Zealand but around the world.

> *Since the 1970s [the] structured approach to writing books for beginners has been heavily attacked. The new* Ready to Read *(1982–86) scheme reflected a world-wide fashion dubbed 'whole language'. Invited authors were told not to be constrained by any word lists or sentence formulae but to set their own 'direct dialogue' ... with young readers. The theory was that 75 percent of English words were so common that they would be mastered easily from unstructured books. 'Learning to read is very similar to learning to talk,' authors were told: it all sounded deceptively reasonable!*
>
> **Beverley Randell**[13]

The new *Ready to Read* 1980s and 1990s ... whole language in action

By the early 1980s the *Ready to Read* series had been in place for 20 years and it was time to revise it. There was a feeling among whole language opinion leaders in New Zealand that the controlled vocabulary of the old series was too contrived. Instead the books should be interesting, authentic literature. New publishers like Wendy Pye, with her *Story Box* and later *Jellybeans and Sunshine* reading series, took the place of those who had produced the old series. With the whole language movement spreading rapidly throughout North America at this time, New Zealand publishers met with phenomenal success there.

The 1985 revision of *Ready to Read* drew heavily on whole language theory, especially the ideas of Marie Clay, Ken and Yetta Goodman[14] and Frank Smith. In the Department of Education's 1985 teacher handbook that accompanied the new reading series *Reading in junior classes*, teachers were told that skilled readers do not read every word, that they sample letters from words in the text, and so on. Good readers learn letter–sound rules through reading, not vice versa. Learning the rules is not necessary at a conscious level; instead it occurs implicitly as a byproduct of reading.

But by 1985 the whole language theory of reading was an issue of heated debate. A number of researchers, here and overseas, were questioning whether good readers sampled the print while reading and whether they used context cues to guess/predict meaning.[15] They argued that these strategies were exactly the wrong ones to use, and were more typical of poor readers than good ones. In many parts of the world there was a growing consensus that early difficulties in phonemic awareness were causing problems in learning to read for many children, and that children's ability to predict and use context cues were not key factors in the learning process. The New Zealand view, which held on to these now shaky assumptions, had become problematic.

In 1985 the *Ready to Read* series was revised, drawing heavily on whole language theory. Teachers were told that skilled readers do not read every word and that they learn letter-sound rules through reading, not vice versa.

Going to the Beach is reproduced by permission of the publishers Learning Media Ltd, on behalf of the Ministry of Education, PO Box 3293, Wellington, New Zealand, © Margaret Mahy, 1984

The revised *Ready to Read* approach

The revised *Ready to Read* materials, published by government-owned Learning Media, remain the staple resource in the reading programme in most schools today. The New Zealand government purchases the *Ready to Read* materials and distributes enough copies for every child to every primary school in the country. In addition, schools can and do buy other reading materials from other companies.

The graded *Ready to Read* series is organised into three basic levels:

- **emergent**, where the reader is just starting to grasp the writing system and the nature of books;
- **early**, where the beginner reader starts to integrate three whole language sources of information: semantic cues (i.e. relevant meaning), grammatical cues (i.e. correct part of speech) and grapho-phonic cues (i.e. sampling of the printed letters of words);
- **fluency**, where the reader's attention to print detail diminishes and the emphasis is on reading for a purpose.

Students are read stories regularly. In shared writing, the teacher models the process of writing and shows children how to spell. The idea is that, through writing and inventing spellings on their own, children learn to listen to sounds in words and link these sounds to letters. Writing (but not reading) is seen as a way of acquiring knowledge of grapho-phonic cues, that is, letter–sound correspondences.

For each of the three basic reading levels, the teacher uses three different teaching approaches. For example, at the emergent phase, when children are first learning to read, the three different kinds of reading involved are: shared, guided and independent reading.

In **shared reading**, children are encouraged to think about what the reading might be about. The teacher reads a book, such as a 'big book', to the whole class. After some preliminary questions, the teacher reads the text virtually straight through, perhaps with the occasional question to encourage children to anticipate what might happen next. Children follow up the shared reading by re-reading the text with the help of a read-along cassette or by reading to each other.

Secondly, in **guided reading** the shared book reading is more in-depth. Children and teacher engage in more detailed discussion of the story before it is read, while it is being read and after it is read. Guided reading is done in small groups. Children are expected to integrate cues during the shared reading. Attention is given to meaning cues, grammatical structure cues and grapho-phonic cues. Children are encouraged to predict the meanings of words and sample the grapho-phonic cues, especially looking at the initial one or two letters, and then check whether their guesses match the initial letters.

With the third approach of the emergent stage, **independent reading**, the child reads without the teacher's help. After taking the child through the first one or two pages of the reader, the teacher lets the child complete the reading of the text. Usually the book is short, predictable and memorable. The teacher is expected to monitor the child's reading, to ensure that the child is 'not left to flounder'.[17]

At the emergent stage children are given a lot of teacher assistance, with instruction given in the context of reading a text. They are expected to become independent learners gradually. In the next stage (early stage), the teacher ensures that the children's predictions are consistent with meaning, grammatical and grapho-phonic cues. When children are able to read accurately and quickly on their own, they are at the fluent stage.

As the above description indicates, whole language does not teach phonics directly. Children can only learn phonics by themselves, working out what sounds the letters represent. Despite the free access that schools have to Reading Recovery teachers and Resource Teachers of Literacy to help failing readers, more and more parents are resorting to private tutoring agencies, for which they are often paying considerable fees, to ensure their children of average ability are saved from failure. Many of these agencies advocate a phonics system of instruction; local schools often regard them with hostility and sometimes discourage parents from using them.

So how successful has whole language been?

The New Zealand establishment has been proud of the apparent success of our reading programmes, which have received worldwide attention and have prompted teachers from all over the world to visit our classrooms. Yet research statistics tell a different story, with international comparisons indicating a decline in reading standards in this country (see chapter 1). We should ask ourselves when our fall from a position of comparative excellence began.

It may be that the decline in standards began after 1981. Before then, reading achievement scores, based on re-checks of the norms for standardised tests used in New Zealand, were remarkably stable. After 1981 no further monitoring was carried out, partly due to cost and partly because new standardised tests were produced, making comparisons with original test results more difficult. During the 1980s the revised *Ready to Read* materials were introduced fully to New Zealand schools.[18] When the IEA survey was carried out in 1990, it found evidence of the decline in reading standards.

From data on today's adult readers, it appears that reading comprehension levels rose between 1930 and 1950 when the systematic phonics approach was in place along with the look and say method. The decline set in after 1970 when whole language began to dominate as the teaching approach.
Alexander Turnbull Library, Wellington. F68959

Another clue to the timing of the decline may be found in comparing the cohort differences in reading comprehension as highlighted by the International Adult Literacy Survey in 1997. If the age groups surveyed are related back to the time when they were at primary school, the overall trends in reading competence seem to match major changes in instruction methods.[19] This analysis suggests that comprehension levels rose between 1930 and 1950 when the systematic phonics approach was in place along with the look and say method, then levelled out in the 1950s and 1960s when look and say and its successor whole language began to supplant systematic phonics. The decline set in after 1970 when whole language began to dominate as the teaching approach.

Thus even without a national assessment or monitoring, the available data suggest a decline in reading standards while New Zealand's education industry has been under the spell of whole language. The failure of our primary schools to teach one child in four to read is the education system's greatest failure because it is from this point that a child's learning journey begins to unravel. Denial is no solution, although it has been tried. In response to an ERO report that damned their leadership and the poor reading levels in their schools, for example, 17 principals paid $250 each for newspaper advertisements that stated the ERO was wrong and that their children could read. Many people relate the problem to social class and certainly middle- and low-income children differ in their reading achievement. Yet such political issues are used to divert attention from more central issues like the actual ways of teaching. Researchers who are critical of whole language are vilified and marginalised, and their research is undermined by those with an opposing viewpoint.

The decline in our reading standards coincides with the introduction of the whole language reading method to the exclusion of phonics. The whole language approach developed in the 1970s and 1980s took a form that was much stronger than the approach taken in the 1960s with the early *Ready to Read* series. In the 1960s *Ready to Read* had some vocabulary control; the readers were graded so that there was no steep learning curve and no need for children to memorise each beginner book. The approach retained some phonics, though it was not taught in a systematic way. In the 1980s, however, the revised *Ready to Read* books were only loosely graded and even the books for very beginners contained words that were hard to 'sound out'. Memorisation was encouraged. By reading and re-reading, children were expected to become good readers. Instead many children became good memorisers and did not learn to read.

Conclusions

The 'reading wars' of the 1990s were a debate about the problems of the whole language approach. This approach was teaching children to guess at words while research was saying that good readers did not guess. It was privileging a generation of children from more affluent homes, who were starting school with good pre-reading skills or who had parents prepared to find tutors to teach them to read. Even children from affluent homes could be let down by whole language if they were unable to teach themselves to read. For their part, children from poor homes were failing in droves.

If whole language is to work at all, higher levels of cognitive skills are required. It is far less effective if children do not come from a 'stimulating' home language environment that provides opportunities to learn the alphabet and develop phonemic awareness. Therefore whole language could not work well for poor children as they lacked the basic pre-reading skills needed to teach themselves to read with this approach. Children of the poor deserve better.

Notes

1 Pinker, S. (1994). *The language instinct*. New York: Morrow.

2 Nicholson, T. (2000). *Reading the writing on the wall: Debates, challenges and opportunities in the teaching of reading*. Palmerston North: Dunmore Press.

3 Price, H. (1987). Reading books and reading in New Zealand schools, 1877–1900. In R. Openshaw & D. McKenzie (Eds.), *Reinterpreting the educational past: Essays in the history of New Zealand education*. Wellington: New Zealand Council for Educational Research.

4 Price, H. (1992). *Schoolbooks published in New Zealand to 1960*. Palmerston North: Dunmore Press.

5 Trevor, R. (1941). *Reading in infant classes: The approach to reading in a group of Canterbury schools, considered in relation to recent developments overseas*. Unpublished Master's thesis, University of Canterbury, Christchurch.

6 Flesch, R. (1955). *Why Johnny can't read*. New York: Harper & Row.

7 Crowder, R.G. (1982). *The psychology of reading*. New York: Oxford University Press.

8 Nicholson, T. (1997, December). *The rise and fall of whole language: What is the evidence?* Paper presented to the Australian Educational Association Conference, Brisbane.

9 Clay, M.M. (1967). The reading behaviour of five-year-old children: A research report. *New Zealand Journal of Educational Studies*, 2, 11–31; p. 30.

10 Cited in Openshaw, R. (1991). *Schooling in the '40s and '50s: An oral history*. Palmerston North: Massey University, Educational Research and Development Centre; p. 69.

11 Cited in Openshaw (1991), p. 53 – see note 10.

12 Randell, B. (1998). *Shaping the PM Story Books*. Gondwanaland Press, Wellington; p. 14.

13 Smith, F. (1975). The role of prediction in reading. *Language Arts*, 52, 305–311; p. 305. See also Nicholson, T. (1997). From ABC to Ready to Read. *Set: Research Information for Teachers*. Wellington: New Zealand Council for Educational Research.

14 Goodman, K.S. (1992). I didn't found whole language. *Reading Teacher, 46*, 188–199; Goodman, Y. (1989). Roots of the whole language movement. *Elementary School Journal, 90*, 113–127.

15 Stanovich, K.E. (1986). Matthew effects in reading: Some consequences of individual differences in the acquisition of literacy. *Reading Research Quarterly, 21*, 360–407.

16 Randell (1998) – see note 12.

17 Department of Education. (1985). *Reading in junior classes*. Wellington: Learning Media; p. 105.

18 Nicholson (2000) – see note 2.

19 Taylor, Rowan. (2001). Submission to the Education and Science Select Committee, 352; point 29–31.

CHAPTER 3

Phonics vs Whole Language – the Issues Behind the Debate

IN THE DISCUSSION OF APPROACHES TO TEACHING OF READING in the previous chapters, I have mentioned the three main ways to teach reading:

1. The **real books approach** (or **whole language** or **literature-based approach**) assumes children will pick up reading by being exposed to books. Children learn to read by being read to, by reading with someone, and by reading on their own.

2. The **look and say method** requires children to memorise the shape or distinctive features of a word in order to recognise the word. Children learn to read by using their visual memory to build a large store of 'sight words'.

3. The **phonics approach** teaches children to identify a word by applying letter–sound correspondence rules to 'sound out' the word. Children learn to read by using a small set of letter–sound rules to sound out the spoken forms of the words.

Most schools use a haphazard mix of the three to teach reading – or so they say. But since the 1970s few teachers have taught phonics in a systematic and enjoyable way. The phonics and look and say approaches have been largely replaced by the more ideological whole language approach that began in the 1960s and grew fully during the 1970s and 1980s. This change has been increasingly questioned in the light of disturbing research evidence on the effects of whole language teaching on literacy levels. The emerging debate focuses particularly on the benefits of phonics teaching over an approach that is based on whole language teaching alone.

The Ministry's official position: 'We do teach phonics'

The official New Zealand position is that the Ministry of Education takes a 'balanced' approach to reading instruction, with an implication that this balance includes the teaching of phonics. The tone of the Ministry's submission to the Parliamentary Education and Science Select Committee brooked no debate as to the rights and wrongs of its position. Its politically correct, hands-off, 'balanced' approach to reading and writing was described as:

> Reading to, reading with (shared reading, guided reading), writing with (modelled writing, shared writing) and independent reading and writing.

Where does this statement suggest that teaching is a professional, highly skilled calling with research evidence supporting its methods? Parents could well be excused for thinking, 'Hey, even I can do that!' Parents themselves work with their children on the activities that the Ministry describes. What concerns them is that they rely on the professionals to do more, and the professionals do not seem to be doing it.

> *Our house is filled with books. My children are read to on a regular basis and are eager to learn. Yet they struggle with the logistics of written language. I am concerned that my children are going to miss the boat and [I] try to back up their efforts at home. But I lack the practical material to do so.*
>
> ***A parent***[1]

And where is phonics? The so-called balanced approach is really about learning to read by reading and writing, and by guessing and predicting, which are key elements of whole language. The approach is not a balance of the main approaches at all. It does not encompass whole language, look and say, and phonics. It is a whole language approach.

According to the Ministry of Education's submission:

> Effective teachers know as much as possible about their children's language and literacy experiences and home values so that they can build on these strengths. They also have expectations that all their students will become readers and writers.
>
> Effective teachers also know that, regardless of how long a student might be in their class ... they can make a difference to that student's progress and achievement in reading.

The words are all very fine but I ask what happens to young teachers, trained in providing lots of fun reading activities and assured that it is by these means and these means alone that children learn to read, who then find they have a group of students with whom the approach just isn't working? When teachers find that their pupils have had very little in the way of 'literacy experiences' at home, what do they do then? Teachers may have 'expectations' that their pupils will learn to read but how does this translate into knowing what to do to ensure every pupil does learn to read?

Also in its submission to the Select Committee, the Ministry of Education addressed the resources available for teaching reading:

> Teachers should have access to a wide range of interesting material ... in a range of media, appropriate to the instructional levels, including repetitive texts, rhymes, poems and songs to enhance children's print and phonological awareness.

Guess where schools get these materials?

> Most schools use the Ministry of Education's materials that are provided to them free of charge, supplemented by material they purchase from commercial publishers ... .The major classroom reading materials provided to schools are produced by Learning Media under contract to the Ministry of Education. Learning Media is a Crown owned company established in 1993, whose shareholding ministers are the Minister of Education and the Minister of Finance.

So Learning Media, as the publisher of the 'free' books such as *Ready to Read*, *Junior Journals* and *School Journals*, is responsible to the Ministry for its budgets and the thrust of the philosophy behind its reading materials. The materials are designed to support a whole language approach, without the close controls on vocabulary that were a feature of look and say materials and without the easily decodable, Dr Seuss-type vocabulary that was in phonics materials. In consequence, a teacher who wants to use a programme with a different emphasis from whole language is going to find it very difficult to get materials from the Ministry even if he or she does have the knowledge at the phonological level to remedy reading problems within the class.

The Ministry of Education supports instruction in reading and writing that involves 'Reading to, reading with, ... writing with ... and independent reading and writing.' Parents could well be excused for thinking, 'Hey, even I could do that!

Ans Westra, 1963. Alexander Turnbull Library, Wellington M541

Phonics in practice: conflicting reports

The Education and Science Select Committee heard conflicting and, at times, diametrically opposed views of what actually happens in relation to the teaching of phonics in New Zealand classrooms.

What colleges of education, New Zealand Educational Institute and Reading Recovery said

Submissions to the Select Committee from colleges of education (teacher training colleges), the New Zealand Educational Institute (NZEI, the union of primary school teachers) and Reading Recovery practitioners claimed that all New Zealand teachers of reading have an element of phonics in their programmes. But it was not at all evident to the Select Committee that this was the practice.

What parents said

To many parents who spoke to the Select Committee, very little phonics instruction is given at the beginning level. Most parents born in the late 1950s probably learned to read in the mid 1960s using *Ready to Read* books and learned from teachers who had themselves been taught in the mid 1940s or early 1950s with the *Janet and John* readers (see chapter 2). Because phonics remained an important element of teaching at that time, these parents have a good sense of what is missing when their children fail at reading and they turn to the professionals for a remedy.

However, when they do seek a way of redressing the problem as quickly as possible, what they get is a more intensive version of what failed in the first place – such as Reading Recovery. Moreover, if the school doesn't admit by the time a child is six that there is a problem, it can offer little else by way of intervention after that. At best the child may receive some well intentioned one-to-one assistance from a teacher's aide.

What the Education Review Office said

In discussing the impediments to good teaching of reading in New Zealand, the ERO submission noted teachers' lack of attention to the development of phonemic awareness in their pupils:

> Teachers quite often fail to include in their teaching programmes work designed to enhance children's phonemic awareness. As a consequence some children may not gain an awareness of the importance of sound patterns in speech and will be less likely to notice these patterns in written language.

The reading debate

In New Zealand as elsewhere the reading debate is still raging, despite the assertion that it is 'tired' and has served its purpose.[2] The debate continues because one child in four still struggles to learn to read. Many parents and hands-on educators find the extent of this failure unacceptable and are determined to do better for these children.

Part of the difficulty in gaining so much as an overview of this debate is that those involved cannot even agree on the terms. I have mostly used the term *whole language* when talking about the approach that predominates in New Zealand as it seems to be the most common. There is, though, wide disagreement about its use. A submission from a lecturer at the School of Education, University of Waikato,[3] described *whole language* as terminology belonging to the practice of teaching in the United States:

> New Zealand teachers have tended to use the word 'integrated' or 'developmental' to describe their approaches which have been located across literary, progressive, psycholinguistic and child development theories ... [They] have used a variety of approaches and have sought to teach to the needs of the child.

Is there support for this view? There are several important arguments to the contrary. First, although different terms (*integrated* or *developmental*) have been used in the past, the New Zealand approach today is associated with the whole language approach. There is virtually nothing to distinguish it from the whole language movement, especially since the early 1980s. To the contrary, the movement has adopted the New Zealand approach as its own. Whole language proponents Ken and Yetta Goodman[4] have written that whole language had its historical roots in New Zealand.

Second, although the New Zealand teacher handbook *Reading in junior classes*[5] advocates a 'variety of approaches', each of these is part of the whole language approach. For example, this 'variety' includes reading to children and guided reading.

Third, although whole language is supposed to teach to the needs of each child, it only does so within the range of activities that are acceptable in the whole language framework. Other activities that may be more helpful in responding to the needs of the child, such as teaching of phonics rules, are not acceptable within the whole language approach. Many of those who defend the current Ministry of Education approach are adept at deflecting the debate on to questions of definition rather than trying to maintain a defence of the indefensible.

These and other issues in the debate over the whole language approach first came to public attention during the early 1990s. In 1993 Jenny Chamberlain wrote the first investigative article on the literacy crisis in *North and South*.[6] A later *20/20* television report by Louise Wallace[7] focused on Doris Ferry, who had been teaching phonics successfully even though local schools did not approve.

In 1995 Noel O'Hare, writing in the *New Zealand Listener*,[8] highlighted several problems with whole language teaching. First, one in four children receive remedial reading tuition at the age of six. Second, trainee teachers are given virtually no instruction in how to teach phonics so they have no alternative ways of teaching reading, even though the ability to vary their approach might reduce the high rate of reading difficulties. Third, children from disadvantaged backgrounds suffer the most from whole language because their parents do not have the 'cultural capital' to overcome the deficiencies of whole language. As we shall see (in the next section below), his points are backed up by research findings. Yet his article provoked outrage when it appeared.

An article by Warwick Roger in *Metro* in 1995 caused more outrage.[9] The first radio programme to cover the reading debate was the Kim Hill Show in 1995; numerous discussions of the 'reading wars' also took place on talkback radio during the 1990s. On Television New Zealand's *60 Minutes*, Janet McIntyre covered the reading debate as it was happening in the United States as well as in New Zealand.[11]

> *[If phonemes] are real they are not necessarily real at a high level of awareness. That is to say, it does not follow from anything I have said that the man in the street can tell you about phonemes, or that he can even tell you how many phonemes there are in particular utterances.*
>
> ***Liberman***[10]

Problems with whole language — the research findings

Research is unearthing the inherent flaws in the whole language system.

It does not acknowledge the crucial role of phonemic awareness

One of the problems for those who are wedded to whole language precepts is that research is beginning to show serious faults in this method. Most researchers now agree that phonemic awareness is crucial in the learning process and that it needs to be explicitly taught where students lack this awareness. Problems with phonemic awareness are characteristic of children who have difficulty with reading. Yet whole language theory has never acknowledged the importance of phonemic awareness in learning to read. Although research in the 1980s and 1990s highlighted the importance of teaching this skill, the Ministry of Education has never produced a test to assess phonemic awareness in children. There are also no materials freely available to schools to teach it directly.

Phonemic awareness is important because, to learn to read, children must learn to segment spoken words in terms of their phonemes. A **phoneme** is a unit of sound in a word that distinguishes it from other words. For example, *p, b, d, t,* are different phonemes because they can be used to make different words as in *p̲in, b̲in, d̲in, t̲in*. Speech does not require a conscious analysis of phonemes so it is unnatural for young children to have the level of phonemic awareness that reading requires. Competent readers can be totally unaware of this complex skill they use daily, hourly even. Yet without phonemic awareness, reading even simple instructions can become a hugely difficult task.

Sounds in spoken words in English are not separate components that are lined up one after the other. They overlap in such a way that we hear information about several sounds at the same time. Yet the overlapping makes it difficult to 'hear' the separate phonemes in words. We can hear syllables quite easily because the overlapping function works within a syllable. For example, the word *rainbow* has two syllables (*rain-bow*). But it is much harder to hear the three phonemes in *rain* (i.e. *r-ai-n*) and the two phonemes in *bow* (i.e. *b-ow*). This ability to break spoken words into their phonemes is crucial in reading because phonemes are represented approximately by the letters of the alphabet. For this reason, too, it is critical that children's hearing is acute and accurate.

A short history of phonemic awareness research

The practice of teaching children about sounds in words dates back to the 16th century. However, research on phonological awareness and reading is much more recent.[12] *Researchers in Russia and the United States in the 1960s were aware that preschool children lacked phonological awareness. Looking back, it seems that the researchers from both countries were united in their realisation that the stumbling block in learning to read was the phoneme.*

Glass theory – Moscow 1960s

Elkonin, a child development researcher at Moscow University, wrote about glass theory. In his view, spoken words for beginner readers were like a transparent glass through which the readers looked at the world. If children could be taught that the glass was there, then they would have phonemic awareness. Elkonin described the written word as 'a model of the spoken word – a model of the word's structure and its principle of construction'.[13]

United States research – Connecticut 1960s

Speech psychologist Alvin Liberman and others tackled the phonological awareness problem in the Haskins Labs at the University of Connecticut. Their speech research there showed that phonemes were not like beads on a string; phonemes overlap rather than existing separately in the speech stream. For this reason, it is difficult for the brain to split phonemes off from spoken words. In 1970 Isabelle Liberman, who was more interested in reading difficulties than was Alvin Liberman, presented a paper that linked phonological awareness with the task of learning to read.[14]

Overseas research – 1960s to 1990s[15]

- *Many children have difficulty with deletion of phonemes. For example, they might find it difficult to answer the question: 'What word would be left if the* s *were taken from the middle of* nest*?' (Bruce 1964, England)*
- *Only 20 per cent of five-year-olds can tap the number of phonemes in words like* ice *(two phonemes,* i-ce*) and* spy *(three phonemes,* s-p-y*). (Liberman, Shankweiler, Fischer and Carter 1974, United States)*
- *Older, poor readers perform significantly worse than younger, average readers in picking the one word out of four that does not follow the same phonological pattern. For example, in* weed, peel, need *and* deed*, the odd one out is* peel *as it ends with a different phoneme. (Bradley and Bryant 1978, England)*
- *Children who become poor readers enter first grade with little or no phonemic awareness. In contrast, children who become good readers enter first grade with much higher levels of phonemic awareness. (Juel, Griffith and Gough 1986, Juel 1988, United States)*
- *Children with high phonemic awareness outperform those with low phonemic awareness on all literacy measures, whether they were taught using a whole language approach or traditional basal instruction. (Griffith et al. 1992, United States)*

In her comprehensive review of the literature on reading, Adams[16] *concluded that the 'evidence is compelling: Toward the goal of efficient and effective reading instruction, explicit training in phonemic awareness is invaluable'.*

Recent criticisms of phonemic awareness research

Some proponents of whole language have questioned the research on phonemic awareness instruction. They claim that training studies have improved phonemic awareness and reading of made-up words, but have not enhanced the ability to read real words in real text.[17] *They argue that training studies have short-term effects that disappear when children are assessed one and two years later. Believing that the problems lie in the home, their solution is for parents to do more to build literate environments. As whole language supporters usually do, they explain that when children do not learn to read with this approach, it is because there is something wrong with the children themselves.*

Other critics of phonemic awareness studies have highlighted design flaws.[18] *In their view, scientific design flaws include lack of random assignment to treatment conditions, failure to control for Hawthorne effects, poor measurement sensitivity, insufficient attention to fidelity of treatment, and inadequately described research samples.*

Meta-analysis: what does the weight of evidence show?

One way to answer these criticisms is to look at the weight of evidence from a large number of studies, rather than get bogged down in the details of particular studies. This overview can be achieved through a statistical technique known as meta-analysis, in which the effects of all the training studies are averaged out to assess their general significance.

From their meta-analysis of training studies, Bus and Ijzendoorn[19] *concluded that the case for training effects from phonological awareness instruction was so strong that about '500 studies with null results in the file drawers of disappointed researchers would be needed to turn the current results into non-significance'. The National Reading Panel, a body of reading experts appointed by the United States government, conducted its own meta-analysis of more than 40 peer-reviewed and published articles that were free of design flaws.*[20] *It found that children's reading was more likely to progress well if it was accompanied by phonological awareness instruction.*

Learning to read is not 'natural'

According to whole language apologists, learning to read is a natural process like learning to speak. For example, Smith and Elley stated, 'Children learn to read themselves. Direct teaching plays only a minor role.'[21] The implication is that the ideal environmental conditions for children in learning to read are the same as those that are ideal for the development of speech.

This assumption is another problem for whole language. If learning to read was natural, then why were writing systems invented in only a few places around the world? Spoken language is natural, a gift of evolution, but reading is not. Spoken language is universal among human communities and originated at least 150,000 years ago. Written language is a cultural invention that is far from universal and its origins go back only about 4,000 years.[22] Children do not need instruction to acquire spoken language but nearly all children need explicit instruction at school in order to learn to read. Only a tiny minority of children learn to read before they start school, and these are almost always children who have received some kind of instruction from their parents or siblings.

If children can learn to read by themselves with only a limited amount of direct instruction, then why do a staggering 20 to 25 per cent of all six-year-old children in New Zealand require expensive, intensive, one-to-one Reading Recovery tutoring even after being immersed in a print-rich environment for one year at school? Why is it that very few children can read before they enter school even though many of them come from homes saturated with print? Reading is simply not natural. To learn its unnatural features, like the alphabet and phonemic awareness, a child needs instruction.

Children do not need instruction to acquire spoken language but nearly all children need explicit instruction at school in order to learn to read.

Chug the Tractor is reproduced with the permission of the author Jenny Giles and the publishers Nelson Thomson Australia Pty Ltd.

Predicting and guessing are not what good readers do

Another flaw in the whole language approach is that learning to read involves identifying unknown words by predicting and guessing. Smith and Elley[23] contend that children 'learn to read with minimal input from the text, predicting and confirming and making sense as they go'. Doyenne of reading in New Zealand, Dame Marie Clay,[24] takes a similar position:

> In efficient rapid word perception the reader relies mostly on the sentence and its meaning and some selected features of the forms of the words. Awareness of the sentence context (and often the general context of the text as a whole) and a glance at the word enables the reader to respond instantly.

This view is well established in the ubiquitous *Ready to Read* series, whose introduction describes reading as 'a constantly repeated process of sampling, predicting, checking, confirming and self correcting'.[25]

Based on such assumptions, in a whole language classroom children are not encouraged to use sounding-out strategies as the first line of attack. Although they are given the strategy of using graphophonic cues as one strategy, they must use it only as a follow-up to confirm their predictions when identifying a new word.[26] As described by Reggie Routman[27] in the United States, some of the main whole language strategies are:

> Skip the difficult word. Read on. Then go back.
>
> Re-read from the beginning of the sentence.
>
> Substitute a word that makes sense.
>
> Look for a known chunk of the word.
>
> Look for picture clues.

Notice anything about these strategies? Not one of them is to 'sound out the word'. If you have ever tried to help a beginning reader to identify a totally unknown word with these fruitless strategies, you may well have become fed up and flummoxed by them. The approach simply does not fit with what research shows good readers actually do. Sounding out words is what good readers do automatically, hardly aware that they are doing it, yet this strategy is not on the Routman list.

Over a number of studies, researchers William Tunmer and James Chapman of Massey University[28] investigated how important prediction is in developing knowledge of specific words and in relation to being able to translate letters and letter patterns into sound (phonological) forms. They found that the ability to recode sounds into letter patterns provides the basic mechanism for acquiring word-specific knowledge. This finding has important implications for educational practice. In particular, guessing as a strategy to teach beginning readers is useless when applied to the exclusion of other strategies.

It is better that children predict the meaning [of an unknown word] from other clues at the outset and use their knowledge of the relationship of letters and sounds for confirmation.

Reading in junior classes, *the guidebook used by most beginning reading teachers in New Zealand*[31]

[T]eaching phonics rules explicitly ... is a difficult, unnecessary and largely fruitless activity.

John Smith and Warwick Elley[32]

An example of letter sensitivity

In one study, good readers were highly sensitive to slight changes in spelling. Good readers aged 11 and 12 years were asked to read passages that contained slight misspellings (e.g. the word sporting *was misspelled as* zporting*). The misspelled words slowed down the silent reading of good readers (their oral reading of these words in text was timed with a stopwatch), indicating that they must have been processing words at a fine-grained level, possibly each and every letter.*

Findings of research by Michael Strange[33]

CHILDREN'S BOOK WEEK
"CHRISTOPHER ROBIN"
Fairy Stories
Nursery Stories
"EPAMINONDAS"
WACKY
BABAR STORY BOOK
BERT THE SPARROW

Compelling research on eye movements reveals that we process the printed word considerably more than whole language supporters would have us believe. From studies using sophisticated cameras that track exactly what the eye looks at while reading, right down to the individual letter, it is evident that word skipping is minimal. The eye fixates on almost every word in every sentence, missing only the most frequent words such as *the*. But when we are fixating on a word, how does anyone know what we are doing? Smith and Elley contend that we might be sampling letters or looking at the general shapes of words.[29] But eye-movement researchers have found that skilled readers seem to be processing words in detail. They notice even slight misspellings,[30] which suggests that words are processed at the letter level. (See more on eye-movement research in chapter 6.)

The weight of evidence supports the view that we recognise words by their letters. The skilled reader is able to process words quickly, at an average of four words per second or 240 words per minute. Context can help to predict words and can be helpful to some extent for function words like articles and prepositions. But it is least helpful for content words like nouns and verbs. Overall, studies have shown that total reliance on context will only help the child to read one word in four correctly.[34] Why would we want to teach children a strategy that only works on average for one word in four? Even when the child uses the initial letters of a word to guess its meaning, context is still not very helpful. Using context also takes time and slows down the reading process. Skilled readers are adept at processing letters in words quickly and without reference to context cues. There is little evidence to support to the argument that they use sophisticated guessing.[35]

Most content words that are high in meaning do not occur often and thus are not readily predictable. How is the child to read these rare words if he or she has never seen them before? Word frequency studies have found that just 100 words account for 50 per cent of all the words we read.[36] Moreover, 5,000 words account for 90 per cent of words in children's reading material.[37] What is significant, however, is that at least 80,000 other words occur in that material – each one of them appearing on only rare occasions, about one or two times per million words. And these infrequent words are the key words of reading, important for understanding all the different texts we read on thousands of different topics. For example, in a text on the discovery of penicillin, the key words are not the high frequency words like *of, was, the, some, by*; instead they are words like *doctor, Alexander Fleming, fever, disease, infection, medicine, germs, antibiotics*.[38] Knowing the most frequent words is obviously helpful and the child will be able to read most words accurately. But these are not the key words. The key words, the ones that carry most of the meaning, are the other 10 per cent of words.

Whole language supporters try to take the moral high ground by saying that their activities aim to generate meaning, understanding and the love of language.
But phonics teaching has the same aim.
Ferguson and Osborn, Alexander Turnbull Library, Wellington. 56596½

Research has shown that the addition of phonics to a whole language classroom produces excellent results.

The Learner as a Reader is reproduced by permission of the publishers Learning Media Ltd, on behalf of the Ministry of Education, PO Box 3293, Wellington.

Thirty to forty years ago the argument for the power of context was generally supported. In an influential study, Ken Goodman[39] found that children read words in context with 60 to 80 per cent more accuracy than in an isolated list. These results convinced Goodman that he should never let children read words out of context again. Other early research on context effects with both adults and children supported Goodman's findings in favour of the importance of context to reading. It took more than two decades for extensive research to build up and overturn these conclusions.

Tom Nicholson conducted a similar version of Goodman's study with New Zealand children.[40] In setting up his own study, however, he recognised some problems with the original Goodman study. Goodman had presented children with the isolated lists first, which gave them practice with reading the words they would encounter in context. Nicholson wondered, would children therefore read words better on a list if they had first seen them in context? He designed the study with the tasks in the reverse order. The results supported his hunch. A graduate student helping Nicholson with the data collection said, 'There must be something wrong with your study. Some children are reading better on the lists.' It turned out that good readers were just as good at reading words whether they appeared in lists or in context. In contrast, poor readers were better at reading words in context as opposed to words in lists even though they also had the opportunity of reading in context before reading the list.

Nicholson concluded that context effects were only applicable to beginner readers and poor readers; they were the ones who had to rely on context cues because they lacked decoding skills. Good readers did not need this crutch to read words. These New Zealand findings received international coverage, for example in United States magazines such as *Science* and *Education Week*. Since then a number of other researchers have found similar results.

Whole language writers often argue that many words are impossible to decode so decoding is not an appropriate strategy in learning to read. In an overseas study, Patrick Groff[41] found that many words can be read successfully with phonics as long as the child uses context as a back-up. He read aloud to children a series of sentences, deliberately mispronouncing a word in each one. In doing so he was simulating the situation where a child has applied phonics rules but does not read the word correctly (e.g. read *find* as *finned*; read *have* as *hayv*). Groff found that 90 per cent of the time, the children identified incorrect words, using the sentence context.

Tunmer and Chapman[42] replicated these findings in New Zealand. Children correctly guessed 25 per cent of the irregularly spelled words without any help from sentence context at all. When given a sentence context for the word, children could guess even more of the words (66 per cent) correctly. More importantly, although children in general were able to identify the irregular words better when they were in sentence context, the children who were most adept in this regard had emerging or good phonological recoding skills. The irregular words were harder for poorer readers to decode, whereas better readers were able to decode more of each word, so had better letter–sound information with which to guess each word. This pattern of results shows that when given the same words to read, good readers read better in context than poor readers, not because they are necessarily better at guessing but because they are better at phonological recoding.

There are better predictors of whether a child will learn to read

Knowledge of the alphabet and phonemic awareness are the two most reliable factors in predicting whether a child will learn to read. Without these two skills on entry to school, a child is at risk of not learning to read. As Tunmer and Chapman's research showed,[43] these two skills have a much stronger influence on later reading performance than any of the numerous other variables they assessed, including socioeconomic status. In addition, knowledge of letter–sound patterns is necessary for both learning new words (including irregularly spelled words) and for using sentence context to identify unfamiliar words.

These findings show up the key assumptions of the prevailing approach to reading instruction in New Zealand as ridiculous. Rather than teaching beginning readers to use sentence context cues as the main way to recognise words in a text, teachers should coach them to decode words first, including by looking for familiar spelling patterns. The children should be encouraged to use context **only** as a back-up to confirm what they think the word is by using the knowledge of words they already have in their heads.

My espousal of phonics brought me into contact with the establishment – 'too old fashioned'. Reading advisers were patronising – one, I recall, upbraided me for teaching the digraph ph *as sounding* f *as in* phone. *He reasoned that students would be confused when confronted with the word* cuphook. *Have you used the word* cuphook *lately? I would teach it* [cuphook] *as a compound word.*

An ex-teacher of reading in secondary schools in the 1970s

Whole language excludes systematic phonics teaching

In defence of whole language, its exponents protest that they do teach phonics. Grapho phonic strategies, they say, are one of the three main types of reading strategies that they teach, along with meaning and structure (or grammar) strategies. They say they teach phonics as and when it is needed.

But at present nothing is in place in the New Zealand curriculum to ensure that phonics is taught systematically. Its use in the classroom is haphazard at best and is totally dependent on the teacher's skill to recognise the need at the right moment for each and every child. How perfect can a teacher be? How does a teacher know if each child in the class has grasped the letter sounds and where they fit into the English system of writing? According to Tom Nicholson's research, beginner readers who listened to audiotapes of stories memorised the stories but did not learn any reading skills. Thus when a teacher is reading a book as a 'whole' to the class, he or she may not convey the salient aspect of reading; the 'whole' may obscure the parts. Novice readers may just think that the teacher is reading them a nice story.[44]

The addition of phonics teaching to a whole language classroom produces excellent results, as research has demonstrated.[45] New Zealand teachers can get good results with some modification of existing programmes to include more instructional activities relating to phonemic awareness, alphabet and word-reading, to supplement whole language activities.

The Ministry of Education will say that teachers are free to adjust and finetune their reading programmes, without assistance from the Ministry. Yet many diligent teachers lack the training and/or the up-to-date information to make the necessary changes to their programmes. Moreover, under this system less effective or less diligent teachers can persist for years with inadequate programmes without their shortcomings being noticed.

What of the claim that whole language produces a love of reading, while phonics is nothing but a turn-off? McKenna and colleagues[46] looked at the effects of whole language on children's attitudes to reading. They thought that some aspects of whole language, such as the emphasis on exposure to good literature, have a positive effect on reading attitudes. Yet they found no advantage for whole language over phonics-type programmes. Where teachers used a mix of approaches, pupils had more positive attitudes to reading. Other researchers have found that children's enjoyment of reading is related strongly to their success in learning to read. Children who struggle to learn to read are less likely to enjoy reading.[47]

What such findings indicate is that phonics is not the 'bad person' that is often portrayed. Children can enjoy phonics as much as whole language.

Phonics — what is it? how do you teach it?

There is a systematic sequence for teaching phonics. The first step is to realise that English spelling has language layers: Anglo-Saxon, Romance languages (Latin and French) and Greek. The most common, ordinary words in English are from the Anglo-Saxon beginnings of English; teaching starts with these patterns. After learning this Anglo-Saxon layer, the beginning reader learns how to decode other layers of English – that is, Latin and French words that have been introduced as a result of the Roman and Norman invasions of England, and Greek words that have been introduced mainly as technical and scientific words.

For phonics to work well, pupils must have phonemic awareness first. We know that children have to 'hear' separate sounds in words before they can learn to associate letters with those sounds. Pre-readers learn to hear individual sounds by listening to the beginning and ending sounds in words. Games like I Spy can help with initial sounds; rhyming games can help children hear final sounds.

Phonics relies on the ability to recognise the letters of the alphabet. Knowing the letters of the alphabet at school entry puts a child at an advantage, as all that is then required is to learn the sounds of the letters. Children learn the letters of the alphabet by practising reading and writing them.

The most important phonics rules are the 40 or so rules of Anglo-Saxon. Children first learn the sounds of the 21 consonants, not their names. Each consonant typically has one sound. The exceptions are *c*, *g* and *y*. The *c* and *g* each have a second, less common consonant sound (*c* can have a /k/ and an /s/ sound; *g* can have a /g/ and a /j/ sound). Some alphabet charts show the two sounds of both these letters. The consonant *y* can also act as a vowel, where it has a couple of other sounds, such as the /ee/ sound in *baby*.

After learning a number of consonant sounds, children learn the most common sound for each vowel. In phonics, you start with the short vowel sound. As soon as children know one or two short vowel sounds, they can read two-letter words like *at, on, it, am*. They can also read three-letter words, where the teacher uses phonogram patterns or rime patterns like *-ot, -un, -in* to make words like *pot, run, tin*. A list of words with the same phonogram pattern is sometimes called a word family because each word has the same pattern (e.g. *at* in *c-at, h-at, m-at, s-at*). One study found that 37 common phonograms generate up to 500 different but frequent words in beginner reading materials.[48]

After three-letter words, children move on to read four-letter words that begin with consonant blends. A consonant blend is a combination of two or three consonant sounds (e.g. *br, cl, fr, st, st, str, tr*) to produce words like *stop, trap, drop*. Next children tackle four-letter words that end with consonant blends (e.g. *s-and, j-ump*).

Long vowel sounds are the next part of phonics teaching. A long vowel sound makes the sound of the name of its vowel (e.g. a long *a* sounds like *ay*, the same as the sound we use to name this letter). The long vowel sound occurs at the end

In support of phonics — the evidence

The National Reading Panel in the United States recently reviewed the research on methods of teaching reading. Focusing on only the studies with sound research practice, they concluded that the weight of the evidence favoured phonics. The examples below give a sense of the kinds of results that have been found.

- *In a study of 285 first-grade children in Houston, Texas, children who received direct phonics instruction were able to read words faster than children who were taught by the whole language, indirect approach. Only 16 per cent of the children in the phonics group did not improve in reading compared to 44 per cent of the onset-rime phonics group (who learned some but not full phonics) and 44 per cent of the whole language group. Children taught with phonics, but not the children in the other two groups, scored close to the national average in terms of decoding ability. (Foorman, Francis, Fletcher, Schatschneider and Mehta 1998, United States)*

- *Among a group of Australian five-year-olds in their first year of school, 38 children had whole language instruction and 25 had phonics instruction. The children who received phonics instruction were significantly better than the other group in reading words and in reading comprehension. (Tunmer and Nesdale 1985, Australia)*

- *Five-year-old children were taken out of class and given instruction in addition to their classroom whole language reading and writing instruction. An experimental group were taught phonemic awareness and simple phonics, while a matched control group did alternative activities, such as matching pictures for meaning (e.g. 'Which pictures are animals?'). A third group got no extra instruction at all. The experimental group were significantly better than the two control groups in decoding skills and in spelling. (Castle, Riach and Nicholson 1994, New Zealand)*

- *Thirty-six poor readers aged nine years were given 10-minute lessons for three or four days a week, over 11 weeks. Children in the experimental group were taught how to use orthographic rimes (e.g.* -eat*) to help them read new words (e.g.* meat, heater*). Children in the control group were taught to use whole language reading strategies (e.g. look at initial letters of a word, read to end of line and guess). The rime-trained readers made significant gains in reading on a standardised test of word reading, equalling a four-month gain in reading age. (Greaney, Tunmer and Chapman 1997, New Zealand)* of two-letter words such as *go, by, he*. It is also signalled in the spelling of a word by a final marker *e*. This 'silent *e*', which has no sound in itself, indicates that the preceding vowel has a long sound, as in *ride, make*, etc.

Finally, children learn the *r*- and *l*-controlled vowel sounds (such as *-ar, or, -all*). They also learn vowel digraphs, which are two-vowel combinations with either one sound (e.g. *ai* as in *rain*; *oa* as in *boat*) or two sounds (e.g. *ow* as in *row, cow*; *oo* as in *book, roof*).

Final *e* patterns can be used as phonograms to generate words with the same pattern. For example, *-ake, -ope, -ine, ame* will generate words like *cake, make, take*; *hope, rope*; *line, mine, fine*; *same, came*.

Phonics teachers over the years have come up with a vast array of ways to teach letter–sound patterns. They have used colour coding, special diacritical marks, songs, hands-on activities, mnemonics, mime ... there are hundreds of different ideas on how to teach phonics. The only clear preference, as supported by research, is that the teacher takes a systematic approach through the sequence of instruction described above.

Notice another crucial difference between this approach and whole language. In the early weeks of phonics teaching, there is often no reading of books. Children learn the sounds of letters, then they sound out three-letter words, four-letter words and so on. There is a hierarchy of learning, moving from the easy rules to the harder ones.

> *A child who learns the code has knowledge that can enable him to read no matter how the semantic, syntactic and pragmatic cues might conspire against him.*
>
> ***C.A. Perfetti, American expert on reading***[50]

Phonics — a lifelong toolkit

As we have seen, since Rudolph Flesch argued for it in 1955,[49] research has continued to confirm the advantages of systematic teaching of phonics. The most recent and arguably the most significant report comes from the National Reading Panel in the United States, the group of independent experts appointed to make definitive recommendations on literacy instruction. As part of its findings from its research review in 2001, the panel promulgated a list of criteria for effective reading instruction. Phonemic awareness and phonics head the list because these are the skills that will ensure any child can read. There is no need to look for extraneous reasons for failure such as a child's race, home life or culture.

> *Without the mnemonic support of the spelling to sound connections, the visual system must eventually become overwhelmed: the situation in which [these children] are left is roughly analogous to learning 50,000 telephone numbers to the point of perfect recall and instant recognition.*
>
> ***Marilyn Adams and Maggie Bruck***[51]

Phonics enables a child to decode most of the half-million words in the English language without ever having heard or seen them before. Once mastered, it gives children a far greater reading vocabulary than rival approaches in which each word must be memorised individually or guessed at.

Through systematic phonics teaching, the child is in effect given a toolkit with which to attack any word he or she may come across – particularly if it is in isolation. It is a foolproof toolkit and is forever applicable. Children who rely mostly on partial visual and sentence context cues at the expense of phonological information remain weak in word recognition because they do not develop such a rich network of written and sound patterns in their lexical memory. They have no toolkit to help unlock the unknown.

Because phonics delivers better readers than the whole language approach alone, we need to consider how to take advantage of this positive aspect of phonics. We need to take action because many children are not learning to read or not progressing as well as they could be. So why on earth is this evidence that phonics can deliver better readers constantly ignored?

Although the concepts of phonological and phonemic awareness may seem theoretical and airy-fairy to grassroots teachers of all viewpoints, their importance is paramount. Whole language advocates need to admit that not all children develop the necessary ability in phonemic awareness simply through immersion in a print-rich environment, and that some children will need direct instruction in phonological awareness.

Although whole language teachers say they teach phonics, what they do is unsystematic, piecemeal and therefore not true phonics teaching. Whole language supporters try to take the moral high ground in the reading debate by saying that their approach focuses on the high-level aspects of reading, using language- and literature-rich activities. The aim of these activities is to generate meaning, under-

Summing up the pros and cons[52]

	Advantages	Disadvantages
WHOLE LANGUAGE	*The early emphasis on literature makes reading fun from the start. Children learn words in context, with a goal of increasing overall understanding.*	*If children 'skip' words, they may never learn them. Teachers often do not fully teach children how to decode the alphabet.*
PHONICS	*Children learn strategies for decoding words they have never seen before. Tutoring may help bring kids with early reading problems up to the appropriate level for their age group.*	*Teachers may rely on 'skill and drill' lessons. The emphasis on decoding practices may turn children off literature.*

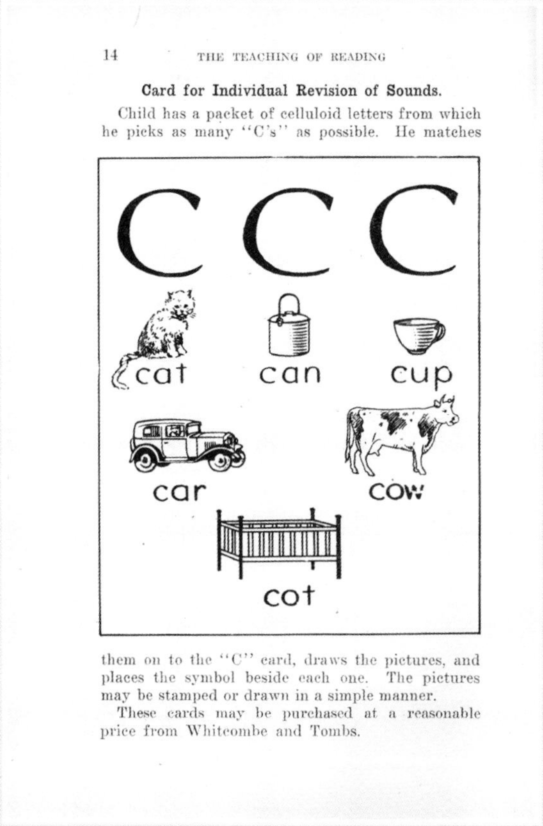
14 THE TEACHING OF READING

Card for Individual Revision of Sounds.

Child has a packet of celluloid letters from which he picks as many "C's" as possible. He matches

them on to the "C" card, draws the pictures, and places the symbol beside each one. The pictures may be stamped or drawn in a simple manner.

These cards may be purchased at a reasonable price from Whitcombe and Tombs.

Before the 1970s, teachers themselves learned how to use phonics systematically in teaching reading. Since then a whole generation of teachers has been taught the whole language approach to reading, with the result that very few know anything about phonics.
Alexander Turnbull Library, Wellington B-K 548-14

standing and the love of language. But phonics teaching has the same aim. No single approach will achieve the high ideals to which it aspires unless every child learns to read. Whole language goals are fruitless if children lack the necessary decoding skills to produce high levels of reading fluency associated with proficient readers. Equally, of course, we do not want children to use decoding skills in a mechanical way as a result of not learning them properly. This kind of outcome is not satisfactory to phonics exponents either. Phonics instruction is grounded in the history of the language. It is just as concerned with language as is the whole language approach, but its concern lies with the phonological forms of language.

The whole language approach, dominant on the stage of New Zealand education for the last few decades, has failed to deliver to all children. Now it must be made to share the stage equally with a phonics approach grounded in phonemic awareness instruction. Explicit phonics instruction should be implemented immediately on entry to school, with the aim of turning children into proficient decoders by the end of the first terms of school. Teachers have to be upskilled, trainees need phonics training, teaching materials and hands-on activities must be produced, and decodable books must be written for phonics children. Parents also need training in what they can do to help. Once children learn to decode, they will be able to access the rich resource of children's literature that whole language advocates want for them.

Conclusions

Children begin their reading development struggling to find distinctive shapes and features of words that will help to remember them. They also rely on memory for the text, sometimes learning it by heart so they can read it just as well without the book. They rely on picture cues and context cues too. But if we provide early instruction in phonemic awareness, children will get off to a better start in learning to read. Rather than wait for phonemic awareness to dawn on the child, we will get better results by teaching children to think about the phonemic form of words as distinct from the content of words. The sooner children realise that words are made up of phonemes, the sooner they will be able to crack the alphabetic code and begin the process of learning the letter–sound rules of English. The child who can use letter–sound rules is able to read words on his or her own, which means that the door to the world of books has begun to open.

Notes

1 Cited in Nicholson, T. (2000). *Reading the writing on the wall: Debates, challenges and opportunities in the teaching of reading*. Palmerston North: Dunmore Press; p. 23.

2 Ministry of Education. (1998). *Report of the Literacy Taskforce*. Wellington: Author.

3 Cawkwell, Gail. (2000). Submission to the Education and Science Select Committee, 38.

4 Goodman, K.S. (1992). I didn't found whole language. *Reading Teacher, 46*, 188–199. Goodman, Y. (1989). Roots of the whole language movement. *Elementary School Journal, 90*, 113–127.

5 Department of Education. (1985). *Reading in junior classes*. Wellington: Author.

6 Chamberlain, J. (1993). Our illiteracy: Reading the writing on the wall. *North and South*, pp. 66–76.

7 Kenna, A. (producer), and Wallace, L. (1995, 24 April). *20/20: War of words*. [Television broadcast] Auckland: TV3.

8 O'Hare, N. (1995, 15 July). What's wrong with reading? *New Zealand Listener*, pp. 18–22.

9 Roger, W. (1995, August). The phonic boom: Adventures in the reading trade. *Metro*, pp. 48–58.

10 Cited from a talk in 1968 in: Bertelson, P. & de Gelder, B. (1993). The emergence of phonological awareness: Comparative approaches. In I.G. Mattingly & M. Studdert-Kennedy (Eds.) *Modularity and the motor theory of speech perception* (pp. 393–412). Hillsdale, NJ: Lawrence Erlbaum; p. 394.

11 McIntyre, J. (2000). *60 Minutes: 'If I woz a dog.'* [Television broadcast] Auckland: TV1.

12 Nicholson, T. (1997). Phonological awareness and learning to read. In D. Corson & L. Van Lier (Eds.), *The Encyclopedia of Language and Education: Vol. 6. Knowledge about language*. Dordrecht: Kluwer.

13 Elkonin, D.B. (1973). USSR. In J. Downing (Ed.), *Comparative reading* (pp. 551–579). New York: Macmillan; p. 561.

14 According to Mann, V. (1991). Phonological awareness and early reading ability: One perspective. In D.J. Sawyer & B.J. Fox (Eds.), *Phonological awareness in reading* (pp. 191–216). New York: Springer-Verlag.

15 These studies are cited in Nicholson (2000) – see note 1.

16 Adams, M.J. (1990). *Beginning to read*. Cambridge, MA: MIT Press; p. 331.

17 See: Coles, G. (2000). *Misreading reading: The bad science that hurts children*. Portsmouth, NH: Heinemann.
Krashen, S. (1999). Training in phonemic awareness: Greater on tests of phonemic awareness. *Perceptual and Motor Skills, 89*, 412–416.
McQuillan, J. (1998). *The literacy crisis: False claims, real solutions*. Portsmouth, NH: Heinemann.

18 Troia, G.A. (1999). Phonological awareness intervention research: A critical review of the experimental methodology. *Reading Research Quarterly, 34*, 28–52.

19 Bus, A.G., & van Ijzendoorn, M.H. (1999). Phonological awareness and early reading: A meta-analysis of experimental training studies. *Journal of Experimental Psychology, 91*, 403–414; p. 411.

20 Ehri, L.C., Nunes, S.R., Willow, D.M., Schuster, B.V., Yaghoub-Zadeh, Z., & Shanahan, T. (2001). Phonemic awareness instruction helps children learn to read: Evidence from the National Reading Panel's meta-analysis. *Reading Research Quarterly, 36*, 250–287.

21 Smith, J.W., & Elley, W.B. (1994). *Learning to read in New Zealand*. Auckland: Heinemann; p. 87.

22 Nicholson (2000) – see note 1.

23 Smith & Elley (1994); p. 142 – see note 21.

24 Clay, M.M. (1991). *Becoming literate. The construction of inner control*. Auckland: Heinemann; p. 8.

25 Ministry of Education. (1997). *Reading and beyond*. Wellington: Learning Media; p. 7.

26 Nicholson (2000) – see note 1.

27 Cited in Pressley, M. (1998). *Reading instruction that works: The case for balanced teaching*. New York: Guilford Press; p. 23.

28 Tunmer, W.E., & Chapman, J.W. (1998). Language prediction skill, phonological recoding ability, and beginning reading. In C. Hulme & R.M. Joshi (Eds.), *Reading and spelling: Development and disorder* (pp. 33–67). Hillsdale, NJ: Lawrence Erlbaum.

29 Smith and Elley (1994) – see note 21.

30 Rayner, K., & Pollatsek, A. (1989). *The psychology of reading*. Hillsdale, NJ: Lawrence Erlbaum.

231 Department of Education (1985) – see note 5.

32 Smith and Elley (1994) – see note 21.
See also: Smith, J. (1997). Whole language and its critics: A New Zealand perspective. *The Australian Journal of Language and Literacy, 20*, 156–162; p. 143.

33 Strange, M. (1977). The effects of orthographic anomalies on reading behavior. *Journal of Reading Behavior, 11*, 153–161.

34 Gough, P.B. (1983). Context, form, and interaction. In K. Rayner (Ed.), *Eye movements in reading: Perceptual and language processes* (pp. 203–211). New York: Academic Press.

35 Adams (1990) – see note 16.
See also: Underwood, G., & Batt, V. (1996). *Reading and understanding*. Oxford: Blackwell.

36 Croft, C. (1997). Write to spell in primary classrooms. In J. Wright (Ed.), *Set Special: language and literacy*, Item 11. Wellington: New Zealand Council for Educational Research.

37 Carroll, J., Davies, P., & Richman, B. (1971). *The American heritage word frequency book.* Boston: Houghton Mifflin.

38 Adams, M J. (1991). Why not phonics and whole language? In W. Ellis (Ed.), *All language and the creation of literacy* (pp. 40–53). Baltimore, MD: Orton Society.

39 Goodman, K.S. (1965). A linguistic study of cues and miscues in reading. *Elementary English, 42*, 639–643.

40 Nicholson, T. (1991). Do children read words better in context or in lists? A classic study revisited. *Journal of Educational Psychology, 83*, 444–450.
See also: Nicholson, T. (1993). The case against context. In G.B. Thompson, W.E. Tunmer, & T. Nicholson (Eds.), *Reading acquisition processes* (pp. 91–104). Clevedon: Multilingual Matters.

41 Groff, P. (1983). A test of the utility of phonics rules. *Reading Psychology, 4*, 217–225.

42 Tunmer, W.E., & Chapman, J.W. (1999). Teaching strategies for word identification. In G.B. Thompson & T. Nicholson (Eds.), *Learning to read: Beyond phonics and whole language* (pp.74–102). New York: Teachers College Press.

43 Tunmer & Chapman (1999) – see note 42.

44 Gibbs, C.J., & Nicholson, T. (1999). When you've heard it all before and still can't read. *Effective School Practices, 17*, 78–84.

45 Tunmer, W.E., Chapman, J.W., Ryan, H.A., & Prochnow, J.E. (1998). The importance of providing beginning readers with explicit training in phonological processing skills. *Australian Journal of Learning Disabilities, 3*, 4–14.

46 McKenna, M.C., Stratton, B., Grindler, M.C., & Jenkins, S.J. (1995). Differential effects of whole language and traditional reading instruction on reading attitudes. *Journal of Reading Behavior, 27*, 19–44.

47 Tunmer et al (1998) – see note 45.
See also: Liu, S. (2000). *Friendships, attitudes toward reading, and reading achievement*. Unpublished Master's thesis, The University of Auckland, Auckland.

48 Wylie, R.E., & Durrel, D.D. (1970). Teaching vowels through phonograms. *Elementary English, 47*, 787–791.

49 Flesch, R. (1955). *Why Johnny can't read*. New York: Harper & Row.

50 Perfetti, C.A. (1991). The psychology, pedagogy and politics of reading. *Psychological Science, 2*, 70–76.

51 Adams, M.J., & Bruck, M. (1993). Word recognition: The interface of educational policies and scientific research. *Reading and Writing: An Interdisciplinary Journal, 5*, 113–139.

52 Adapted from Hancock, L.N., & Wingert, P. (1996). If you can read this ... you learned phonics or so its supporters say. *Newsweek*, p. 75.

CHAPTER 4

Reading Recovery and More Effective Intervention Alternatives

EVEN WITH THE BEST PRACTICE IN EVERY CLASSROOM, THE Literacy Taskforce has agreed, effective intervention programmes will still be needed for children who benefit from more intensive specialised teaching. Current interventions that provide specialist assistance include Reading Recovery, Resource Teachers of Literacy, Resource Teachers of Maori and Resource Teachers of Learning and Behaviour.

But do the resources supplied to these programmes represent money well spent? Are the interventions helping children to make long-term progress? In the case of Reading Recovery, the scientific research says no. For other intervention programmes there is no clear evidence either way. In this chapter we focus on Reading Recovery because it is the programme on which research evidence is available.

An overview of Reading Recovery

The major literacy intervention in New Zealand schools is Reading Recovery. It is designed to enable underachieving six-year-olds to reach average reading levels for their class through daily, one-to-one reading tuition. Up to 25 per cent of six-year-olds receive Reading Recovery tuition each year. Nearly 300 full-time equivalent teaching positions are allocated to this programme. It costs $18 million annually.

In *Shaping the PM Story Books*, Beverley Randell describes how she has used the New Zealand colour system for describing the difficulty level of books; and how the information provides the equivalent Reading Recovery levels. *Shaping the PM Story Books* is reproduced with the permission of the author Beverley Randell and the publishers Gondwanaland Press.

Origins

Marie Clay at The University of Auckland designed Reading Recovery during the late 1970s. She researched the programme in a number of Auckland schools with the support of the District Inspector of Schools. The initial results were phenomenal, indicating that children in the programme could, after a relatively short period of tuition, reach the average level of reading of their classmates and could continue to make progress at an average level after they returned to the classroom. During the 1980s the Department of Education began to implement Reading Recovery throughout the country, starting in Auckland and Hamilton.

The appeal of Reading Recovery was that children with reading difficulties could be identified relatively early and given an intervention that would put them back at the same level as their classmates. By the mid 1990s Reading Recovery was in place in 70 per cent of schools and was reaching 14,000 six-year-olds annually.

Access

To gain entry to Reading Recovery, children are assessed for reading progress at the end of their first year of school, at six years of age. A child who is not making progress in reading will be considered for Reading Recovery. The only constraint is that each school can select no more than 20 per cent of its six-year-olds for tuition.

The lessons

The tuition consists of daily lessons of about 30 minutes in length, for an average of 12 weeks. During the lesson, conducted one-to-one with a trained Reading Recovery teacher, the child mainly reads text material and writes a story about the text. The reading strategies are consistent with the whole language approach. The child is taught to predict, guess what the word means and confirm the guess through looking at the first (and last) letters. There is no sounding out of words as in phonics (see chapter 3). Part of the lesson might be to break words into 'sounds' to help with spelling. The teacher records the child's reading behaviours during the lesson, taking a 'running record' to ensure that the reading material is not too difficult. Teachers implement the same programme all over the country.

Reading Recovery 'research'

In the initial years of its implementation, Reading Recovery appeared to meet with such amazing success it seemed hard to argue against making it available to all New Zealand schools. Yet the claims to success were based on research designed in a way that was not typical of scientific research.

In science studies, the usual procedure to test a new product is a randomised trial where participants are randomly assigned either to the experimental group or to a control group. The developers of the product usually leave the research activities to others who, ideally, do not know which is the experimental group and which is the control group. The control group is given a 'placebo' so that its members think, like the experimental group, that they are getting special treatment.

This approach was not taken in the Reading Recovery trials. Children were not randomly assigned to an experimental group. Instead, schools selected children for the experimental group on the basis that they were the ones who needed most help. The control group was not randomly selected either. It comprised another group of children who were not achieving as well as their classmates on average but were progressing better than the experimental group. Because the control group was above the reading level of the experimental group, the two groups were not matched at the start of the study. In addition, in contrast to the experimental group, the control group received no special attention (that is, no placebo).

The problem with a non-randomised trial is that it is impossible to know the real reason for any positive results found – they may be due to the Reading Recovery tuition or to some other factor, such as the children's feeling that they were getting 'special treatment' (called the 'halo effect') or the special enthusiasm of their Reading Recovery teachers. It is a weak design in science because there is no level playing field from the start. However, it is a common design in education. It is difficult to do randomised experiments when you are dealing with schools in which the needs of the child take precedence over concerns for an appropriate experimental design.

A more significant weakness was that the study was not an independent evaluation as it was carried out by Reading Recovery staff. The Department of Education did not conduct an independent evaluation of Reading Recovery until the mid 1980s when the national implementation of the programme was well underway.

Independent evaluations of Reading Recovery

In 1986 Ted Glynn and others at Otago University were commissioned by the Department of Education to carry out an independent evaluation of Reading Recovery in the Otago–Southland region. The results, released in 1989, were negative.[1] They suggested that the high initial gains in Reading Recovery 'washed out' once children were discontinued from the programme.

A weakness of the study was that, like the original Reading Recovery study, it did not conduct randomised trials. The researchers thought it would be unethical to randomly assign children in need of instruction to a control group because that would mean they would miss out on extra instruction. Therefore the control group comprised those children who were not eligible for Reading Recovery but were at a low reading level. The total sample from 12 schools was 83 children, with 42 children in Reading Recovery and 41 in the control group. Each Reading Recovery child was assessed on entry to the Reading Recovery programme. At the same time, a control child was also assessed. Each pair of children was then assessed several further times over a two-year period. Unfortunately, children began and finished Reading Recovery at different times during the first year so at each assessment period different numbers of children were in each group.

The first assessment, for a group of 21 children who had reached 'discontinuation' (i.e. the end of the programme), showed that Reading Recovery children were reading at the same book level as the control group, even though they had started at a lower level. From pre-test (before the programme) to post-test (after discontinuation), the Reading Recovery group gained almost 11 book levels (from 4.1 to 14.7), while comparison children gained only six book levels (from 8.5 to 14.5).

At the next assessment, at the end of the year, the Reading Recovery children were still nearly two book levels ahead of the comparison children (16.7 versus 15.1). However, when assessed in the first term of the next year, Reading Recovery children had slipped two book levels behind the control group (16.6 versus 18.8). When assessed in the second term, they were about 1.5 book levels behind (18.9 versus 20.5). When assessed in the third term of that year, they were two book levels behind (20.5 versus 22.7).

These results should have raised alarm over the effectiveness of the programme. Instead the Reading Recovery teacher training team criticised the study itself. According to Roger Openshaw at Massey University, who used information from the National Archives, Reading Recovery coordinators did not accept the findings and did not want the results to impede the programme's implementation.[2] Their unpublished criticisms may have had some effect as the implementation of Reading Recovery continued with little impact from the Otago report. At about this time, too, Reading Recovery was being adopted overseas, starting with the state of Ohio in the United States. From the late 1980s it was implemented in Canada, the United States, Australia and the United Kingdom.

By the late 1980s and early 1990s New Zealand and overseas academics were asking questions about the design problems associated with Reading Recovery research. In 1989 Tom Nicholson wrote a critique of the Reading Recovery research design in the *New Zealand Journal of Educational Studies*;[3] a similar critique had been reported in a United States journal.[4] Bill Tunmer in 1990 raised questions about the effectiveness of Reading Recovery,[5] to which Marie Clay responded, disputing his arguments.[6]

In a review of Reading Recovery research in the mid 1990s, Shanahan and Barr[7] concluded that it was effective but not as dramatically successful as had been claimed by its supporters. They argued it was an expensive intervention, which might be made more cost-effective. Iversen and Tunmer[8] found that the per-pupil cost of Reading Recovery could be reduced with the addition of phonological awareness, simple phonics and learning of high frequency 'sight' words. With these 'phonics' additions, children reached the same reading levels in a third less time than normal. From a meta-analysis of one-to-one tutoring programmes, Elbaum and colleagues[9] concluded that findings 'do not provide support for the superiority of Reading Recovery over other one-to-one reading interventions.' In view of these results, they observed, 'It is particularly disturbing that sweeping endorsements of Reading Recovery still appear in the literature.' Hiebert, on reviewing the research on Reading Recovery, also questioned its value for money in terms of overall effectiveness.[10]

During the 1990s Bill Tunmer and colleagues[11] at Massey University conducted a second independent evaluation of Reading Recovery. In a longitudinal study, they and others followed 152 children from the Manawatu in the North Island through their first three years of school. In the second year, 26 of the children completed the Reading Recovery programme. Their progress was compared with a group of 98 children who did not receive Reading Recovery. The results showed that the Reading Recovery children never caught up to the control group, even when tested a year after they completed Reading Recovery.

Another finding of the study was that reading and spelling skills were insufficiently developed through Reading Recovery. The children were tested at the end of 1993 and mid-way through 1994, by which time all the Reading Recovery children had completed the programme. On a test of invented spelling, the Reading Recovery children made considerable progress, moving from a score of 16.8 to 38.2, but they were still behind the comparison group, who had moved from 43.9 to 53.4. The word reading scores of the Reading Recovery children had moved from 4.2 to 11.7 on a standardised Word Reading Test, but the comparison group had moved from 21.8 to 32.3.

One interpretation of these data is that the Reading Recovery children had been discontinued too soon. They had graduated from the programme before they had caught up to their classmates in reading and spelling. Another interpretation is that the Reading Recovery programme was not effective enough. It was not able to give these children the reading skills they needed to catch up with their classmates.

Can we do better than Reading Recovery?

Of course we can do better than Reading Recovery – if we want to. More effective alternative interventions, as assessed through sound research, are available. A now considerable database shows that key factors in the effective treatment of reading disabilities are explicit instruction in phonemic awareness, followed by explicit, systematic instruction in phonics combined with extensive practice in reading decodable text, where words can be easily sounded out.

The recent 2001 report of the National Reading Panel in the United States was clear that such instruction is more effective than whole language instruction. There is also evidence that Reading Recovery itself can be modified and improved. Iversen and Tunmer[12] found that Reading Recovery supplemented with systematic phonics was 37 per cent more efficient than Reading Recovery alone. In a study comparing five treatments for reading problems, Wasik and Slavin[13] found that two programmes, both providing explicit systematic phonics and extensive practice in reading decodable texts, were much more effective than Reading Recovery. Similarly, Hatcher and colleagues[14] reported that adding systematic training in phonological awareness to a remedial programme modelled after Reading Recovery was highly effective and produced greater gains in the poor readers than did either the remedial programme or phonological awareness training on its own.

Several studies in the 1990s showed the significance of phonological processing skills to both initial reading difficulties and progress in Reading Recovery. White and colleagues[15] found that children in Reading Recovery were particularly weak in phonological processing skills. The children who benefit from Reading Recovery are likely to be those who start the programme with relatively high levels of phonemic awareness, while those who start with low levels of phonemic awareness derive little or no benefit, as at least two studies have shown.[16]

Recommendations for future interventions based on research

The development of phonemic awareness in non-readers stands out as the single most important feature of successful intervention programmes. Numerous studies[17] have supported this thesis.

In the United States, Foorman and colleagues[18] found that explicit, systematic instruction in sound–spelling relationships in the classroom reduced reading disabilities better than a print-rich environment, even with children who had benefited from phonemic awareness instruction in kindergarten. Conversely, as with many other studies, teaching children to use context and prediction as strategies for word recognition resulted in more reading disabilities than did instruction in use of sound–spelling knowledge as the primary strategy.

In the same study, changing instruction from whole language to explicit, systematic phonics at the classroom level reduced the occurrence of reading problems more effectively than any of the three types of one-on-one tutorial programmes evaluated in National Institute for Child and Health Development intervention studies. The researchers concluded that to avoid reading failure, the focus should be on prevention, not intervention.

> *[Explicit, systematic instruction in sound–spelling relationships] brought economically disadvantaged, low-achieving first and second graders close to the national average in reading, whereas whole language instruction placed these students near the 25th [percent]ile. Children scoring below the 25th [percent]ile are often identified as reading disabled under traditional diagnostic criteria.*
>
> **Barbara Foorman and colleagues[19]**

What is wrong with Reading Recovery?

Reading Recovery has not fulfilled government expectations that it will help nearly all children learn to read. At best the programme brings a child to the average level of his or her class, no matter what the overall achievement level of the class is. At worst it repeats more intensely the teaching patterns that have failed in the first place, increasing a child's sense of failure and frustration and lowering his or her self-esteem in regard to academic achievement still further. Even if a child is considered to be 'successful' in Reading Recovery terms, his or her 'recovery' is not sustained during the following years of schooling.

Some of the specific criticisms directed at Reading Recovery are outlined below.

1. **Reading Recovery helps fewer students than is claimed.** Reports that 75 to 85 per cent of the children in Reading Recovery are successful are misleading because 'successful' does not mean the children are readers. It only means they have reached the average level for their class. In many low-decile schools, the school average is below the national average. So even if children are at their class average, they can still be failing to read.

Moreover, no one knows how many children in Reading Recovery are successful in terms of more meaningful literacy levels. The Ministry of Education has never published standardised test data on the success rates of children who have completed the programme.

2. **Children initially successful in Reading Recovery are often not successful later.** As mentioned above, two longitudinal studies (in Manawatu in the 1990s[20] and in Otago in the 1980s[21]) found that Reading Recovery children did not maintain their initial progress once they returned to the classroom. Instead they immediately fell behind and continued to lose ground steadily until they were no better than classmates who also needed help with reading but did not receive Reading Recovery.

3. **The system of reporting Reading Recovery data is flawed.** Reading Recovery practitioners report significant success. But the people who are responsible for 'success' collect the data to prove their success. In 2001 the Ministry of Education finally required Reading Recovery tutors to submit information on children's reading progress. Why did it take so long? And will the data be made public from now on?

   Even if the data are published, they will be hard to interpret as they contain two problems: content bias and unequal intervals between levels. In the case of content bias, the Clay Diagnostic measures sample the specific skills taught in the Reading Recovery programme. That is, what is taught is what is measured. Assessments emphasise reading tasks and skills that are unique to Reading Recovery tuition. The children in the control group may have little experience with the kinds of tasks evaluated by these measures, while Reading Recovery children have had extensive experience as a result of their reading lessons. Comparisons on these measures are likely to exaggerate the amount of learning for Reading Recovery children.

   In regard to the second flaw, unequal intervals between reading levels, the primary evaluation tool in the Clay Diagnostic measures is the book-level measure, which is used to place each child in one of the 20 levels of the programme booklets. It is the only measure in the battery that requires the children to read connected text. Though the text is connected, it is not the kind of text that children normally read; rather, it is 'predictable' text, where pictures and repetitive sentence patterns prompt the reader. At the final 20th level the text is least predictable, but children generally do not reach the 20th level before they are discontinued as they need to reach only the class average (usually level 16) to be returned to their classroom.

4. **Access to Reading Recovery is not fair to children living in poor areas.** The administration of Reading Recovery is formulaic, inflexible and inequitable. Sectors of society and schools in certain areas get a lower level of access than others even though their needs are arguably greater.

When students are six years of age, the school checks on their progress by administering the Clay Observation Survey. A school team of experts (in consultation with parents) recommends the most deserving cases for inclusion in the programme. The daily individual tuition is supplementary to the classroom programme. When the child is judged suitably 'remediated' (after 12 to 20 weeks), he or she is returned to mainstream classes.

The process of selecting children for Reading Recovery is far from exact. Schools differ in their view of what 'falling behind' in reading is. Some consider it to apply to six-year-olds in the bottom 5, 10 or 15 per cent of readers in their peer groups. In other schools, children from the bottom 20 to 25 per cent of readers are considered to be falling behind.

Reading Recovery's goal is to bring the pupils with the lowest reading levels to the average level of their class. Some of the children at the lowest levels will be brought up to only the average of what may already be a low-performing class. Statistics show that schools in poor areas of New Zealand (called 'low-decile' schools) are overrepresented in poor performance of reading. Hence this inequity of access impacts on poor children.

5. **Not all children have access to Reading Recovery.** In 2000 there were 12,061 children (21 per cent of the total six-year-old population) in Reading Recovery programmes.[22] Of these, 9,138 (16.2 per cent of all six-year-olds) entered the programme during 2000, while the remainder continued on from 1999. Yet Reading Recovery coverage of schools has been declining, as has the number of children entering primary schools. In 2000 Reading Recovery was available in only 69 per cent of schools, which together covered 82 per cent of pupils. Based on these figures, the proportion of children in Reading Recovery in 2000 was 25.6 per cent of the six-year-olds for whom it was available.

That is, 25.6 per cent of children were considered to be 'falling behind' in 2000. And as there are many small schools that do not even participate in the programme (only 47 per cent of schools from the North Island Central East district had Reading Recovery in the year 2000), we can assume that there are still a lot of children needing help who aren't getting it – or at least not from Reading Recovery!

6. **Reading Recovery is expensive.** In 1999, 260 full-time teacher equivalents were available nationally to assist state schools to run the programme. This provision was set in the 1980s and has been maintained at the same level ever since. Reading Recovery is currently funded by direct support from the Ministry of Education and indirect support from the schools. The direct costs in 1999 were $18 million. The Ministry of Education estimated that between 30 and 52 per cent of the total cost of Reading Recovery resources is met through schools' discretionary funding.

   Thus it is easy to see why the schools from poorer areas have lower participation in the programme. To fund their pupils' participation, schools have to take from other needed resources. According to Ministry of Education estimates, the cost per child is $14 for each session if only the direct resource costs are used or somewhere between $21 and $27 for each session if indirect resources from schools' general operations grant are also included. Despite this huge amount of funding, the Ministry has not spent anything on independent evaluations of the costs and benefits of the programme, except for two one-off studies in the 1980s and 1990s. Many have agreed that Reading Recovery is not cost-effective.

7. **Low-decile schools miss out on Reading Recovery.** Schools with the heaviest load of underachieving children are losers in the spread of allocation of Reading Recovery funds. The data on access to the programme were analysed according to school decile rating for the first time in 1999. It turns out that in 1999 the proportion of low-decile schools with Reading Recovery was lower (65 per cent for decile 1 schools and 63 per cent for decile 2 schools) than the proportion of high-decile schools with Reading Recovery (81 per cent of decile 10 schools). Yet more children from low-decile schools (19 per cent) were entering Reading Recovery than those from high-decile schools (15 per cent from decile 9 and 13 per cent from decile 10).

   If more schools in the low deciles were able to access Reading Recovery for all the children who were considered to need it, how many more children would be in the programme?

8. **Urban—rural access to Reading Recovery is not balanced.** Reading Recovery is more likely to be available in schools in main centres than in rural schools. Yet in 1999 rural schools had proportionately more of their children (19 per cent) in Reading Recovery than did urban schools (16 per cent). Sixty per cent of schools in New Zealand have fewer than 100 pupils each. Many of them do not have the same access to Reading Recovery that urban schools do even though they have greater needs in terms of children who need help with reading.

Criticisms in submissions to the Select Committee

Submissions that schools made to the Parliamentary Education and Science Select Committee reiterated the inequity of the spread of Reading Recovery. A Manurewa school[23] echoed the views of others in its submission that:

> Reading Recovery should be allocated on a needs based allowance. There should not be a differentiation between areas with some children in higher socio-economic areas being moved into Reading Recovery at levels ten and eleven, when we have children missing out on this programme in other [socioeconomic] areas and yet they are operating at levels zero and one. Is it fair to allow some children to miss out on a chance for literacy because they attend a decile one school in Manurewa rather than a decile ten school in Remuera?

In its submission, the Education Review Office had similar concerns, which were in summary that:

- Reading Recovery provides for the weakest readers in a class, whether that class is in the most affluent area in the country or in the poorest area, rather than providing for the weakest readers in the country as a whole;
- it has not resulted in equitable outcomes for students nationally. Large differences between the best and the worst readers remain;
- its long-term effectiveness is open to question;
- children with low letter–sound awareness benefit least. Reading Recovery does not correct this deficiency.

We have substantial data to prove that the overall level of children's literacy at age six in a decile one school is significantly lower than that of the overall level of literacy of children in a decile 6 to 10 school. These data are based on the Diagnostic Survey administered to all children at the age of six. Yet Reading Recovery hours are disseminated on the grounds of school roll. We have had our hours for Reading Recovery cut with a roll drop and yet this school has always had to leave children out of the programme because there weren't enough spaces.

Deputy principal, Raumanga School, Whangarei, submission to the Select Committee

Other criticisms

In the late 1990s the government appointed a Literacy Taskforce, mainly composed of school practitioners. Like many of those making submissions to the Select Committee, the Taskforce expressed a concern that high-decile schools had more teachers trained in Reading Recovery than did low-decile schools. The Taskforce also raised several important issues about the programme itself:[24]

- Children with the greatest need should be targeted, particularly in low-decile schools.
- The stage at which Reading Recovery is delivered could be more flexible.
- Cultural understanding by Reading Recovery teachers is an important element of the teaching of Maori children.
- A literal translation of an English intervention programme is inappropriate for Maori-medium education, where children first learn to read in Maori.

The government-appointed Literacy Taskforce raised concerns about the Reading Recovery programme, especially in regard to its effectiveness in reaching and meeting the needs of those children most in need of it.

- Children with specific learning difficulties have needs that cannot be met through Reading Recovery.
- Only two independent research studies have been carried out on the programme in New Zealand independently of the monitoring and research by those running the programme. This number is insufficient to identify any trends indicating the need for refinements or improvements.

A Literary Experts Group, commissioned by the Ministry of Education to advise the Literacy Taskforce, agreed to:

> ... [r]ecommend that Reading Recovery places greater emphasis on explicit instruction on phonological awareness and the use of spelling-to-sound patterns in recognising unfamiliar words in text.[25]

Theoretical weaknesses in Reading Recovery

Marie Clay designed Reading Recovery to help low-achieving six-year-olds to catch up in reading. The concept of an early intervention programme was innovative in the late 1970s. The problem is that the programme was modelled on whole language theory, a theory that is now widely regarded as wrong. Most researchers today would totally disagree with Clay's statement that 'in efficient rapid word perception the reader relies mostly on the sentence and its meaning and some selected features of the forms of words.'[26] To the contrary, they would argue that efficient reading relies mostly on the ability to process the forms of words. In Reading Recovery, however, teaching the child to sound out words is not done systematically because it is not seen as a major part of efficient reading. Instead, the child is taught to focus on meaning clues, a strategy that researchers during the 1980s and 1990s have discovered is characteristic of a beginning or poor reader, not a good reader (see chapter 3).

Clay argued that children need to acquire the ability to use multiple cues to solve problems while reading and to engage in the specific strategies of cross-checking, predicting and confirming. She specifically stated that children should be discouraged from relying too heavily on word-level cues, warning that children's attention may be diverted from comprehension and an understanding of the language structure 'when instruction directs students to conscious manipulations of letters, sounds, or single words'.[27]

This neglect of cues at the letter–sound and word levels is now seen as the main problem with Reading Recovery. It stresses the importance of using information from many sources without recognising that skills and strategies involving phonological information are crucial in learning to read and write. Instead of doing something different to the approach of the regular whole language classroom, Reading Recovery does the same thing, except one-to-one.

What we have in New Zealand is a situation where children do not learn phonics strategies in the regular classroom and do not learn them in Reading Recovery either. This situation is not acceptable. There are clearly more effective alternatives. In practical terms, it can be argued that Reading Recovery is a programme that is too late for many at-risk students. Research shows that children at high risk for reading failure can be identified on entry to school. The two best predictors of reading success (and failure) are knowledge of the alphabet and phonemic awareness. Children who test poorly on these measures at school entry are at risk and best helped through immediate intervention. A structured programme of systematic phonemic awareness and phonics is the best hope that many of these children have to become successful readers.

The case against Reading Recovery

There are too many counts against Reading Recovery for it to continue in its present form. Here is the scorecard against Reading Recovery:

1. Far fewer students than it is claimed actually benefit from Reading Recovery.
2. The benefits of Reading Recovery are short term and do not last. As a result, Reading Recovery does not improve overall levels of school achievement.
3. Reading Recovery is more likely to benefit children who already have phonological awareness.
4. The research on Reading Recovery is flawed. Research by its implementers indicated highly positive outcomes but their research designs were problematic. Independent evaluations have shown much less positive results.
5. Research-based alternative interventions that include more phonics are more effective than is traditional Reading Recovery.
6. Reading Recovery does not provide systematic instruction in letter–sound correspondences (the alphabetic principle).
7. Reading Recovery does not use decodable text, in which the words have letter–sound correspondences that the children have learned as well as a limited number of sight words that have been systematically taught. Decodable text allows children the opportunity to practise letter–sound relationships they have learned in class while reading these words in the context of a story or article.

8. Reading Recovery uses predictable text that leads children to use context cues contained in the pictures and provided by the repetitive sentence patterns instead of using sounds for the letters in the word. Predictable text does not give children the opportunity to practise their letter–sound knowledge in the context of real reading.

9. The system of reporting Reading Recovery data is flawed.

10. The standard for successful completion of Reading Recovery is not equitable, especially for children in low-income and rural areas.

11. Children who are not expected to be successful are sometimes removed from the programme and from the calculation of the success rate.

12. Reading Recovery does not reduce the need for other compensatory reading services.

13. Reading Recovery is extremely expensive, is not effective in the long term, and does not save other costs.

A last word from a parent — and my conclusions

A parent asked in her submission to the Select Committee on reading:

> Why doesn't Reading Recovery work for all children? Why do schools not offer alternative assistance if Reading Recovery fails? Why are schools not held accountable if they fail to teach the basic fundamentals of education?

These are questions we should all put to the bureaucrats and advisers who have decreed that New Zealand six-year-olds, having been denied reading instruction that focuses on basic skills such as phonological decoding, are offered only Reading Recovery by way of intervention – even though the research sends clear alarm signals that Reading Recovery is not working. Will the bureaucrats take care of these thousands of young casualties of a failed intervention? Who will be accountable?

Questions and answers about Reading Recovery

Q. Does Reading Recovery produce gains in reading for students in year one who have reading difficulties?

A. Yes, but only at first. Any initial advances that these students make in their reading ability as a result of Reading Recovery soon disappear.

Q. Is Reading Recovery based solidly on the relevant experimental research findings on reading development?

A. No. To the contrary, Reading Recovery is a projection of the empirically unverified whole language approach to literacy development. Its principles and practices are very similar to those of whole language. Whole language has been shown clearly to be a failed instructional innovation (see chapter 3).

Q. Is Reading Recovery the best remedial reading tuition programme now available?

A. Probably not. The theoretical base to Reading Recovery is inferior to that of other tutoring programmes that incorporate the practices shown by experimental research to be effective. Empirical evidence in this regard, gained from disinterested, independent studies comparing Reading Recovery with competing tutoring programmes, is badly needed if this question is to be answered satisfactorily.

Q. What are the major reasons why studies of Reading Recovery conducted by its advocates always find that Reading Recovery is highly effective?

A. These investigations typically do not compare Reading Recovery with competing tutoring programmes. In action, these studies often have been designed and implemented, either expressly or incidentally, so that they result in favourable outcomes for Reading Recovery. Of note here: when disinterested researchers study Reading Recovery, it is found to be ineffective, especially in the long term.

Q. Is Reading Recovery in its present form, as prescribed by Clay,[28] the most desirable intervention programme?

A. No. It is clear that Reading Recovery must modify the practices that Clay originally established so that the programme conforms more closely with the features of beginning reading development as identified by experimental research. Reading Recovery is over 20 years old. It must be updated.

Notes

1 Glynn, T., Crooks, T., Bethune, N., Ballard, K., & Smith, J. (1989). *Reading Recovery in context*. Wellington: Department of Education.

2 Openshaw, R. (2002). The social and political contexts of early intervention programmes: A case study of Reading Recovery. In P. Adams & H. Ryan (Eds.), *Learning to read in Aotearoa New Zealand* (pp. 81–93). Palmerston North: Dunmore Press.

3 Nicholson, T. (1989). A comment on Reading Recovery. *New Zealand Journal of Educational Studies, 24*, 95–97.

4 Shanahan, T. (1987). [Review of the book, *Early detection of reading difficulties*.] *Journal of Reading Behavior, 19*, 117–119.

5 Tunmer, W.E. (1990). The role of language prediction skills in beginning reading. *New Zealand Journal of Educational Studies, 25*, 95–114.

6 Clay, M.M. (1991). Reply to Tunmer. *New Zealand Journal of Educational Studies, 26*.

7 Shanahan, T., & Barr, R. (1995). Reading Recovery: An independent evaluation of the effects of an early instructional intervention for at-risk learners. *Reading Research Quarterly, 30*, 958–996.

8 Iversen, S.A., & Tunmer, W.E. (1993). Phonological processing skills and the Reading Recovery programme. *Journal of Educational Psychology, 85*, 112–126.

9 Elbaum, B., Vaughn, S., Hughes, M.T., & Moody, S.W. (2000). How effective are one-to-one tutoring programs in reading for elementary students at risk of reading failure? A meta-analysis of the intervention research. *Journal of Educational Psychology, 92*, 605–619; p. 617.

10 Hiebert, E.H. (1994). Reading Recovery in the United States: What difference does it make to an age cohort? *Educational Researcher, 23*, 15–25.

11 Tunmer, W.E., Chapman, J.W., Ryan, H.A., & Prochnow, J.E. (1998). The importance of providing beginning readers with explicit training in phonological processing skills. *Australian Journal of Learning Disabilities, 3*, 4–14.

12 Iversen & Tunmer (1993) – see note 8.

13 Wasik, B., & Slavin, R.E. (1993). Preventing early reading failure with one-to-one tutoring: A review of five programs. *Reading Research Quarterly, 28*, 178–200.

14 Hatcher, P.J., Hulme, C., & Ellis, A.W. (1994). Ameliorating early reading failure by integrating the teaching of reading and phonological skills: The phonological linkage hypothesis. *Child Development, 65*, 41–57.

15 White, C., Fletcher-Flinn, C.M., & Nicholson, T. (1999). *Queensland Journal of Special Education*.

16 Center, Y., Wheldall, K., Freeman, L., Outhred, L., & Mcnaught, M. (1995). An evaluation of Reading Recovery. *Reading Research Quarterly, 30*, 240–263.

Iversen & Tunmer (1993) – see note 8.

17 For a review of the research on phonemic awareness and phonics see: National Reading Panel. (2000). *Teaching children to read: An evidence based assessment of the scientific literature on reading and its implications for reading instruction*. Washington, DC: National Institute of Child Health and Human Development.

For **shorter reviews**, more closely related to New Zealand, see:
Nicholson, T. (1997). Closing the gap on reading failure: Social background, phonemic awareness and learning to read. In B.A. Blachman (Ed.), *Foundations of reading acquisition and dyslexia: Implications for early intervention*. Mahwah, NJ: Lawrence Erlbaum.
Nicholson, T. (1999). Literacy in the family and society. In G.B. Thompson & T. Nicholson (Eds.), *Learning to read: Beyond phonics and whole language* (pp. 1–24). New York: Teachers College Press.
For **specific studies**, see:
Ball, E.W., & Blachman, B.A. (1991). Does phoneme segmentation training in kindergarten make a difference in early word recognition and developmental spelling? *Reading Research Quarterly, 26*, 49–66.
Byrne, B., & Fielding-Barnsley, L. (1991). Evaluation of a program to teach phonemic awareness to children. *Journal of Educational Psychology, 83*, 451–455.
Cunningham, A.E. (1990). Explicit versus implicit instruction in phonemic awareness. *Journal of Experimental Psychology, 50*, 429–444.
Lie, A. (1991). Effects of a training programme for stimulating skills in word analysis in first grade children. *Reading Research Quarterly, 26*, 234–250.
Lundberg, I., Frost, J., & Petersen, O.P. (1988). Effects of an extensive program for stimulating phonological awareness in preschool children. *Reading Research Quarterly*, 23, 267–284.
Vellutino, F.R., & Scanlon, D.M. (1987). Phonological coding, phonological awareness and reading ability: Evidence from a longitudinal and experimental study. *Merrill Palmer Quarterly, 33*, 321–363.
Yopp, H.K. (1988). The validity and reliability of phonemic awareness tests. *Reading Research Quarterly, 23*, 159–177.

18 Foorman, B.R., Francis, D.J., Beeler, T., Winikates, D., & Fletcher, J.M. (1997). Early interventions for children with reading problems: Study designs and preliminary findings. *Learning Disabilities: A Multidisciplinary Journal, 8*, 63–71.

19 Foorman et al. (1997) – see note 18.

20 Tunmer et al. (1998) – see note 11.

21 Glynn et al. (1989) – see note 1.

22 Kerslake, J. (2001, June). Annual monitoring of Reading Recovery: The data for 2000. *The Research Bulletin*, No. 12, 65-71.

23 Finlayson Park School. (2000). Submission to the Education and Science Select Committee, 37.

24 Ministry of Education. (1999). *Report of Literacy Taskforce*. Wellington: Author.

25 Ministry of Education. (2000). *Literacy Experts Group report to the Secretary of Education*. Wellington: Author.

26 Clay, M.M. (1991). *Becoming literate: The construction of inner control*. Auckland: Heinemann; p. 8.

27 Clay (1991); p. 321 – see note 26.

28 Clay (1991) – see note 26.

CHAPTER 5

New Zealanders Have Their Say – Submissions to the Select Committee

IN 1999 THE PARLIAMENTARY EDUCATION AND SCIENCE SELECT Committee agreed to my proposal to conduct an Inquiry into Reading. The Inquiry began in 2000 and its report was published in August 2001.[1] The Select Committee asked those making submissions to the inquiry to:

- examine any matters to do with teaching and learning of reading in New Zealand schools, and in particular the view of educators, researchers, parents and others on how and why many children are failing to read effectively.
- provide recommendations to the Government on how the reading gap can be closed.

The Select Committee was criticised in several quarters for initiating yet another inquiry into reading. In 1998 the National government had established a Literacy Taskforce, and it was advised by a Literacy Experts Group, which the Ministry of Education appointed in the same year. The Taskforce had already defined the country's literacy goal and advised on ways of attaining and measuring progress. Yet the criticisms of the Select Committee for launching a further inquiry showed a misunderstanding of its role and focus. The Select Committee reports to the people of New Zealand via the House of Representatives; it therefore is intended to represent a broad range of perspectives and experiences.

By contrast, the two previous reports had spoken to and reflected the views of those with vested interests in the education system. The teachers, teacher trainers and bureaucrats who already influenced policy decisions on reading instruction were also the authors of the Literacy Taskforce report. The Literacy Experts Group, although containing a mix of those who supported the present system and those opposed to it, similarly was limited to university academics, the New Zealand Council for Educational Research and college of education lecturers. Its final report at least had the benefit of access to research evidence on reading. The report reflected the academic divisions within the group, raising major concerns over the system in some parts but in other parts making low-key suggestions for only minor tinkering with the present system.[2]

The Education and Science Select Committee was aware that the climate of growing public concern about reading standards, which initiated the establishment of the Literacy Taskforce, remained strong. In the 1990s the media, academics and others in the community had raised questions over the mainstream rhetoric that New Zealand had the best reading standards in the world. These questions were still to be answered satisfactorily. Reading Recovery statistics showed that more than one in four children were struggling with reading after their first year at school (chapter 4). The Education Review Office had also published damning statistics about low levels of Maori and Pacific Island student achievement in reading (chapter 1). In response to the enormous concern over literacy standards, the Select Committee gave the public – the ordinary people, parents and frontline teachers – the chance to have their say in the debate. Everyone, it seems, is an expert on reading because everyone has been to school and therefore has some experience – good or bad – of learning to read. By making the Inquiry into Reading its first inquiry of the 2000–2002 parliamentary term, the Committee conveyed the importance of this issue and its recognition of reading as a core learning activity.

Three-hundred-and-sixty submissions to the Select Committee came from a variety of people and organisations throughout the country. All had some form of experience of the practice of teaching reading in New Zealand. All felt passionately about what they had to say.

All is (by and large) well — the whole language camp

Everything is well in the world of reading instruction in New Zealand ... according to submissions from people and institutions with a heavy investment in proving the success of reading instruction based on the whole language approach. For many years now colleges of education, literacy advisers, teachers' unions and the Ministry of Education have defended the status quo. In the past, some university academics have also been strong supporters of whole language. The submissions to the Select Committee were predictable in this regard:

- Some studies 'revealed that our children are amongst the best in the world providing strong support that a holistic, child centred approach benefits the vast majority of our children' – from literacy staff at the Christchurch College of Education.
- For most New Zealand children, 'current child centred practices work well when they are implemented properly' – from teacher educators at the Dunedin College of Education.
- New Zealand has a strong reputation in the field and its current practices 'such as the whole language approach to teaching reading, which acknowledges the place of both phonics and semantics, should not be tampered with lightly' – from the Wellington Literacy Association.
- 'There is no evidence of systemic failure, and our best readers have for decades ranked among the best in the world' – from the Ministry of Education.

This group of submissions representing whole language academics, teacher educators and other vested interests in the status quo can be summed up as being focused on teachers and resources. Cocooned by their theories and preconceptions about what teachers ought to do, these submitters didn't dare look critically at the real world. When faced with shortcomings, they automatically resorted to fixing them up by demanding more of the same things – more Reading Recovery, more books, more inservice training, more specialists and (what all of these boil down to) more funding. In defending the status quo, these submissions acknowledged the 'unfortunate' tail of failing readers revealed by the international studies. They then castigated these victims for their predicament. The very group that most needed help was brushed aside as being only a minority. Children were blamed for being poor readers because of the circumstances that identified them: gender, ethnicity, socioeconomic status and a mother tongue other than English.

Professor Emeritus Warwick Elley from the University of Canterbury used the evidence from the 1990 IEA survey to prop up his assertion that 'by and large, New Zealand children do read well'. Yet how comfortable do you feel with 'by and large'? Professor Elley himself acknowledged the hefty reading gap between the top and bottom 25 per cent of students. Certainly the IEA survey showed that New Zealand had the best readers in the world. However, we also came top in two other much less laudable results: we had the widest variance from the standard deviation (i.e. the spread of scores around the average score) of all OECD countries in the 1990 IEA survey and the greatest gap between the bottom and top 25 per cent of readers (see chapter 1).

Nonetheless, like his fellow proponents of whole language, Elley was keen to emphasise success:

> New Zealand has proportionately more 'good readers' (in the top quarter internationally) than any other country … . On average New Zealand pupils achieved in the top four nations (out of 32) at age 14,

Education and Science Committee
Inquiry into the Teaching of Reading

SUBMISSION

Rowan Taylor
May 2000

A nation of literate children today is the key to our future.

Rowan Taylor's submission to the Select Committee Inquiry into the Teaching of Reading

Just 18 months after switching to systematic phonics, Don Buck Primary School in West Auckland – a decile one school with a high proportion of non-Pakeha and children learning English as a second language – saw the illiteracy rate among its six year olds fall from 40 per cent to zero.
Sunday Star Times, 19 August 2001

and the top six nations at age nine. At both levels New Zealand was the highest scoring English-speaking nation. (Except for the USA at age nine which had a suspect sample.)

Talk about putting a spin on the figures! Yes, New Zealand was the highest scoring English-speaking nation in the survey of 32 countries at age 14 but the survey included only three English-speaking countries (the United States, Ireland and New Zealand) and the English-speaking Canadian province of British Columbia. Moreover, whether the British Columbian sample was representative of all Canadians is difficult to judge; in the PISA literacy survey reported in 2001 (chapter 1), Canada as a whole scored ahead of New Zealand.

What was most worrying about the 1990 survey was the disquieting gap between our best and worst performers in reading. This gap had **not** been evident in the earlier 1970 survey. In his submission to the Select Committee, Professor Tom Nicholson at The University of Auckland explained how the introduction of whole language philosophies into the reading curriculum in the 1980s meant that teachers had to change their methods drastically and teacher trainees were inculcated in a new way of teaching. The unexpected effect of the system, he argued, may have been to privilege the best readers and disadvantage the worst readers.[3] In other words, the rich got better at reading and the poor got poorer.

Predictably, and in line with Elley's contentions, the New Zealand Educational Institute (the union of primary school teachers) defended New Zealand's standards of teaching reading. For support it quoted student performance on the 1996 National Education Monitoring Project survey as 'approximately 80 percent at or above the levels regarded as normal for their year at school'. However, as Rowan Taylor pointed out in his submission, this claim hinges on the word 'normal'. If a normal reader is now reading at standards lower than a normal reader in earlier decades, then we can take no comfort from this finding. How different it is in the United States, where the National Union of Teachers admitted years ago that the country had a reading problem and acknowledged the need for a phonics approach to solve it. That union has commissioned reading experts to bring the latest research to its members. It has lobbied the government and is still working to make improvements.[4]

As the response in the United States highlights, this is not a time for complacency. In their study of 152 Manawatu children, Tunmer and colleagues showed that in addition to the 21 per cent of children in Reading Recovery, 13 per cent were only slightly better at reading.[5] That is, 34 per cent of New Zealand children may be achieving poorly in reading – a proportion even worse than the 20 to 25 per cent figure often cited.

Also giving no cause for complacency are the results from the International Adult Literacy Survey.[6] The survey showed that over 40 per cent of Pacific peoples and 50 per cent of unemployed people function at level one – the lowest level of reading ability. According to the Ministry of Education, people at this level may experience considerable difficulty in reading everyday material such as a newspaper or bus timetable or in making simple calculations such as working out interest on savings. Sixty per cent of Maori, 70 per cent of unemployed people and 40 per cent of employed people function below level three. Among those in employment, the poorest levels of literacy are in the manufacturing, construction and agriculture industries – all with close to 50 per cent of workers at level one. It is going to be an uphill battle to build a knowledge economy from such a low base.

The IALS [International Adult Literacy Survey] results for New Zealand indicated that almost half of adult New Zealanders (over one million people) are below the minimum level of literacy competence required to effectively meet the demands of everyday life and work. Two hundred thousand adults function at the lowest level of literacy, Level one.

Ministry of Education[7]

Some acknowledgement of the problem

'There is a minority of pupils,' Professor Warwick Elley wrote in his submission, 'mostly Pacific island, Maori and Pakeha from disadvantaged backgrounds attending decile one schools, who need more help than they are getting.' In reality, a good indicator that someone is having difficulty with reading is being a Maori boy in a low-decile school where reading instruction is based on the whole language approach. Of course, as part of the overall school population, Maori are in the minority. But once the large numbers of Pacific Island children, and Pakeha children from disadvantaged backgrounds, are included in the assessment of poor reading levels, even Ministry of Education officials have to acknowledge that the statistics:

> ... do highlight a wide variation in performance of reading tasks of particular groups of New Zealand students. ... [D]ata from the IEA survey of reading of nine year olds in 1990 showed that there is a significant difference between the average performance of Maori and Pacific Island students and others. A sizeable gender difference in favour of girls exists across all ethnic groups but Maori and Pacific boys perform significantly below their female counterparts.

Elley's views on why some children are failing, echoed by others, show up the biases of many in the whole language camp. For five-year-olds, he says, with 'good role models at home, plenty of suitable books, fluency in oral language and competent teaching, the complex task of learning to read continuous English prose is manageable and often enjoyable.' Conversely the students who are 'at risk' lack good role models at home:

> [T]hey rarely see adults reading, or valuing books, at home. They have not been read to, and they have not been helped enough with their oral language development to be able to move easily into reading for meaning. They often come to school hungry, upset by family problems and their absentee rates are excessive.

> *The gaps are not a product of a general programme which can be conveniently labelled as phonics or whole language. The general causes are as much to do with our history of colonisation, immigration, and current distribution of resources as they are to do with specific instructional practices. However, instructional practices can make a difference.*
>
> ***Professor Stuart McNaughton***

These sweeping generalisations are insulting to the many parents who value reading yet see their children struggle with it. More than that, he rests his arguments on anecdotal evidence of teachers and Reading Recovery specialists – not on hard evidence. Yes, there are many homes where reading is not valued, where parents struggle to survive let alone read, yet these are not the only homes where there are children who cannot read.

The other group Elley identifies as prominent in New Zealand's 'failure' statistics are the children who have a mother tongue other than English. Our 'literacy gaps', he says, originate from decile one schools that have large numbers of such pupils. Yet many children with parents who speak a different mother tongue, themselves were born in New Zealand and speak English as their first language. It is not simply that their reading is held back because they come from homes where mum and dad do not speak English.

It is as if the whole language reading experts have thrown in the towel before the fight has even begun. While acknowledging that the gaps in reading ability 'are becoming more noticeable, and urgent', Elley claims that 'many problems lie outside the school's reach'.

According to the American Federation of Teachers, scientists estimate that 95 per cent of children can be taught to read at a level constrained only by their listening and comprehension abilities. Some schools in New Zealand have already proved that this assertion is true. Just 18 months after switching to systematic phonics in 1996, for example, Don Buck Primary School in West Auckland – a decile one school with a high proportion of non-Pakeha and children learning English as a second language – saw the illiteracy rate among its six-year-olds fall from 40 per cent to zero. At the same time the school's PAT scores rose, not just in reading but in all subjects.[8] This is the experience of just one school, of course, but it sets a vision of what might be achieved if we made a dramatic change toward teaching of phonics.

> **Researchers have found that in general:**
>
> - *teachers have a greater influence on learning than do parents or other background factors;*
> - *the socioeconomic status of the school has far more impact than the socioeconomic of the child;*
> - *time spent practising skills is a more reliable indicator of achievement than socioeconomic background;*
> - *having English as a second language is no barrier if the child undertakes a systematically developed and carefully implemented English reading programme before the age of six.*
>
> ***Rowan Taylor, Christchurch writer and parent, submission to the Select Committee***

Consistent with others in the whole language camp, the NZEI (quoting Professor Stuart McNaughton) asserted that for many Maori and Pacific Islands children:

> ... these differences [in reading ability] in turn are linked to poor health, inadequate housing, low family income and unemployment. Government policies can make a profound difference to language and literacy practices ...

It also associated the problem with lack of access to early childhood education, which is most likely to be the experience of 'children of families where at least one parent is Maori, where there is a low family income, or where there is no parent employed'.

The convenience of such views for their proponents is highlighted in the submission of Graham Crawshaw, who runs phonics-based remedial 'reading camps' north of Auckland, which he claims have been raising the literacy levels and self-esteem of 'at risk' boys since 1991. He challenges the 'academic elite's' continued determination to shrug off the obvious:

> When top educationalists like Warwick Elley assure me ... that New Zealand is near the top of the literacy tree I feel that he and I must be on different planets.
>
> Essentially I say that the whole language approach to reading favoured by Warwick Elley, Marie Clay, Stuart McNaughton, Libby Limbrick and their loyal proteges (... who control the training colleges) has done the damage.
>
> They say there is no real problem with literacy in New Zealand, that our children are doing fine at reading, Wendy Pye is on her throne and all's well with the world.
>
> ... Our most powerful influential educationalists blame poor reading on medical conditions, the effects of poverty, transient lifestyles, large class sizes and the number of children with English as a second language. Of necessity all their guns are pointed outwards, because it would be just too costly and embarrassing to make themselves accountable for their poor results.

Sir, — One thing Maori parents want is for their children to be able to get good jobs. And this means being able to read and write, which my children in standards 2 and 3 [seven to nine-year-olds] can hardly do. This is not because they have no brains or come from an unhappy home, or are underfed or unloved. It is not because of any other condition teachers usually blame. The children have just not had enough teaching. No wonder Maori children get bitter. What chance have they got? Every complaint made to the school brings such answers as 'Don't worry about it' or 'They'll probably come right all of a sudden.' But how can they if they do not get enough teaching and there is too much talking and fooling in the classroom?

'Angry Maori mother'[9]

Suggested solutions from the whole language camp

Where the whole language camp acknowledged problems, they proposed solutions that focused on teachers and resources and retained the whole language approach, regardless of the growing body of evidence that identifies it with the problem. For example, Elley recommended:

- the provision of more books;
- extension of the use of videos like Wendy Pye's *Magic Box*;
- one-to-one tutoring, giving decile one schools more access to resources such as Reading Recovery;

> *[I]t would be poetic justice if Elley and Co ever need and can't find a literate plumber to fix a hot water cylinder. Recently I saw a memo on the wall of my Dargaville plumbing supply shop that would be funny if it wasn't tragic. It said: 'You are probably aware that there are many people in the market place, tradesmen included who can't read a wiring diagram included with the non-simultaneous booster cylinders. To make it easier for you to explain the wiring and operation to these people I have come up with the attached drawing. ...'*
>
> *Graham Crawshaw*

- a delayed start to formal instruction, on the grounds that many five-year-old boys in particular are too immature physically to sit still and concentrate (however, see the evidence that boys' behaviour in class, not their readiness to read, is the cause of the problem);[10]
- book floods for pupils for whom English is a second language, most of whom lack sufficient exposure to comprehensible print in English.

Similarly, literacy staff at the Christchurch College of Education recommended that:

- an investigation should be conducted to identify what constituted the effective practice of schools achieving higher levels of literacy than might be expected for their socioeconomic status;
- children who are not ready for school at age five should be identified and given oral language enrichment programmes;
- the Inquiry into Reading must recognise the broader and more substantial issues of reading instruction rather than reduce it to a simple discussion regarding the merits of phonics over whole language;
- programmes should be provided for fluent readers at all levels of the school;
- further teacher education is required to enhance reading programmes using a literature-based approach;
- more official recognition should be given to the vital role parents play in the development of their children's reading;
- all student teachers should take a compulsory course in a critique of theorists' views of reading instruction and in working with low-progress children.

Harold Shepherd, a senior lecturer in reading from Massey University, suggested the following actions could 'confidently be expected to narrow the gap between average and below average readers':

- Keep class sizes small in early years of school. Reinstate the 1:20 ratio for years one to three.
- Increase the resourcing for Reading Recovery and the Resource Teachers of Literacy programmes.
- Reduce pressure on teachers by keeping the curriculum manageable.
- Teachers in training need more work in reading.
- More resources should be given to inservice training.
- More New Zealand–based research about the teaching of reading should be commissioned.

For their part, teacher educators from the Dunedin College of Education recommended that additional teaching resources should be allocated to children with difficulties. The Wellington Literacy Association echoed this view, specifying that funding should be directed towards established programmes such as Reading Recovery, Resource Teachers of Literacy and inservice training. Both groups argued that the initiatives stemming from the Literacy Taskforce report needed time to develop fully.

In their submissions, Reading Recovery teachers drew on anecdotal evidence that there is a decline in the oral language accomplishments of children on entering school. They urged that records be kept of ethnic, gender and socioeconomic factors to provide a basis for further research. They stressed the importance of follow-up teaching once a child has been returned to the mainstream and they supported inservice development of teachers. (Here they might as well admit, as research has proved, that any beneficial effects that accompany Reading Recovery do not continue beyond the short term.) Reading Recovery is already effective, they claimed; its continuation is fundamental to 'closing the gap' and its funding should be increased. They also recommended lowering the pupil:teacher ratio in junior classes and increasing the number of social workers in decile one and two schools to address problems of transience, health and absences.

After endorsing the Literacy Taskforce's recommendation regarding refinement of teaching strategies, approaches and materials, the NZEI made predictable teacher-focused recommendations such as:

- increasing professional development opportunities for teachers of 'at risk' groups;
- developing programmes that recognise cultural backgrounds;
- lowering class sizes;
- improving access to and the quality of early childhood teaching;
- addressing the problem of transient children;
- providing national coordination of interventions;
- increasing the number of Resource Teachers of Literacy to work with children;
- supporting programmes like Books in Homes;
- increasing numbers of literacy advisers in schools;
- closely reviewing and assessing all preservice education courses on teaching children to read.

As the industrial and professional organisation of primary teachers, the NZEI has as part of its role the function of providing advice to its 32,500 members on the latest research findings. A curious feature of its submission, therefore, was that it never once referred to the important research work on phonemic awareness that began to emerge in the 1990s. Moreover, when it finally, albeit briefly, addressed James Chapman's claim that the scientific community has rejected the whole language approach, it could not refute the claim convincingly. After quoting vaguely from John Smith's article 'No one way to achieve literacy', it slid off into an argument that anyway the Literacy Taskforce did not argue for replacing whole language with phonics. Of course it did not. However, the very first recommendation of the Literary Experts Group was that teaching should enable children to develop phonemic awareness and phonological recoding skills when they confront unknown and difficult words in text.[11] Guessing strategies and use of sentence context, which are the staple strategies taught through the whole language approach, do not even begin to fulfil this requirement.

Teachers need to understand the absolute importance of phonemic awareness and how to teach it systematically. The NZEI submission comes nowhere near recognising this need when it quotes from the ERO report on literacy that 'teachers use every available tactic in teaching reading including phonics to help students decode and gain meaning from print'. As the ERO report itself goes on to explain, good reading teachers that ERO staff observed emphasised the look of the letters and sounds when they were pronounced (grapho-phonics). A **good** (i.e. not every) new entrant teacher uses alphabet practice to teach letter and word sounds to students. When students come across a word they don't know, they are encouraged to:

> ... look at an initial sound, look at an end sound, look at any medial sound they might recognise, approximate the unknown word according to its word content and approximate the unknown word according to its pictorial context.

But this approach is not the same as teaching systematic phonics. It is phoney phonics. There is a world of difference. In a systematic phonics programme, children move through a hierarchy of learning from the easy rules to the harder ones (see chapter 3).

Support for a phonics alternative

Other submissions to the Select Committee told a different story to the generally positive tale advanced by whole language camp. In contrast to the whole language proponents, these submissions looked at the crux of the matter. Namely, their concerns centred on the way reading is taught and the rigid ideology that underpins the practice in New Zealand.

Views from researchers and practitioners

The central issue, Keith Greaney of Massey University stated, is the kind of strategies that teachers give children to use when they encounter an unfamiliar word. The whole language philosophy has only managed to continue by ignoring the research evidence that poor phonological processing deficits are the major cause of reading failure. Frontline teachers are not to blame because their trainers and advisers have not made them aware of the problem. In his own research,[12] Keith Greaney found teachers do as they are told to do in Ministry of Education publications: they teach whole language strategies of guessing words from picture cues and context. They do not teach phonics. He recommended an investigation, based on a national sample of teachers, to gather further information on the strategies that teachers encourage young readers to use.

Before any real change can take place the classroom teacher must first be convinced that there is a problem, because at the present time, this problem is not evident to the teachers themselves.

Keith Greaney, Massey University

In her submission to the Select Committee, Bonnie Le Grice, head of the Special Education Centre at the Christchurch College of Education, stated that the Centre had assessed and taught to read 200 children between six and twelve years of age from a range of primary schools. She concluded from her experience that children from all social and ethnic groups, and from both public and private schools, are failing to learn to read. In addition, failure to learn to read is not necessarily related to a child's cognitive ability.

On the basis of its assessment, the Special Education Centre divides children into three broad groups:

1. those who can guess words from the context and explain the story;
2. those who cannot guess words from the context and cannot explain the story;
3. those who can read the words but cannot explain the story. (There are very few children in this group.)

In line with other research evidence, the Centre has found that poor readers most commonly are unable to work out a word if there is no picture cue, hear the patterns of sounds in words (phonemic awareness), say the sounds in spoken words, blend the sounds to say the words, make inferences in a story, sequence events in a story or understand the meaning of relative pronouns or referents. Le Grice identified the following reasons for children's failure to make progress in reading at school:

- Teachers do not know about phonemic awareness or phonics, or how to teach them.
- They interpret the whole language approach narrowly.
- Many teachers do not know about the phonic basis of the relationship between reading a word and spelling it.
- Children are left to discover words and meanings for themselves.

- Many children are given books that are too difficult for them to read easily because there are too many unknown words in the story.

According to David Whitehead, a senior lecturer in language education at the University of Waikato, even good readers are failed by the system in that they are prevented from reaching their full potential as fluent, thinking readers. Constraints on their progress include wasted resources (especially the costly Reading Recovery scheme), inadequate teacher training, and wasted instruction time because of administrative demands on teachers. He associated children's failure to read with 'poor teaching, failure to innovate, failure to apply research and thus the dual-coding explanation of the reading process as well as the lack of any definition as to what reading comprehension is'. In his view, to close the gap we will have to 'leave our philosophical egos at the door'. Among the pedagogical changes he suggested are the introduction of new teaching approaches and improving teachers' skills in the use of basic instructional approaches.

Among several other reasons for reading failure, an experienced classroom teacher with SPELD training identified a child's developmental factors at school entry and the system's failure to cater for individual learning styles. In addition, targeted help misses many children who would most benefit from it. In this teacher's view, Reading Recovery, the whole language programme and assessment and diagnostic methods are inadequate, as is the arrangement whereby teacher aides rather than the skilled specialists (teachers) work with children who have the greatest needs. She was also concerned that teachers and schools often are too late in acknowledging a child's reading failure because they are afraid that they will upset parents and/or that the parents' efforts at home will cut across their own work.

In her submission, Anne Stercq of the Seabrook McKenzie Centre, who has assessed over 1,500 students with reading problems, stated that the strategies of the present system (mainly predicting from context, and recognition of first sounds and whole words through repeated exposure) were too limited. Major problems she identified were a lack of flexibility, the attitude that 'one size fits all' in regard to intervention, and poor monitoring and poor reporting of reading progress (the latter shortcoming being frustrating to parents).

One who knows her subject in promoting systematic phonics instruction is Doris Ferry, a reading consultant and campaigner for universal literacy. She learned how to teach phonics before the whole language approach became standard in the system. In her submission she wrote that different children need different approaches. Using phonics does not mean that comprehension is ignored; rather it means that 'those taught thorough phonic skills and sight vocabulary have their minds freer to concentrate on meaning when reading'.

Scornful of the prevalent attitude that reading failure is caused by socioeconomic factors, culture or having a mother tongue other than English, Doris Ferry described her students as:

> ... very normal, well cared for children who had failed in Reading Recovery or other remedial programmes. These children had come from an environment of books in the home, and being read to.

Instead, she attributes reading failure directly to the whole language philosophy's rejection of the one skill that is critical to reading – phonics. She warned against reinventing phonics and introducing 'gimmicky, non-standard and inferior systems from overseas' or just adding 'some perfunctory phonics alongside the current whole language reading books'.

Speaking from personal experience

A huge number of people who made submissions to the Select Committee either had suffered from reading failure or were parents of children who did. Many of their stories of desperation before finding a solution were heart-rending. Equally, however, they showed a determination not to be overwhelmed by the dogma that was spouted by the experts to whom they had turned for advice and help. Although solutions varied, all had one striking feature in common: finally the failing reader was able to make letter–sound connections. This group of submissions covered the following reasons for why children were failing to read:

- Schools fail to recognise the problem early enough, gloss it over and/or deny a problem ever existed.
- Schools and teachers are ignorant of children's different learning patterns and the need for alternative methods of instruction.
- Schools are underfunded and those resources they do have are wasted on Reading Recovery and teacher aides that have not helped.
- Teachers are inadequately trained in theoretical knowledge of reading pedagogy and diagnosis of problems.
- Good systems for monitoring children's reading progress are lacking.
- The whole language approach is unsuitable for some learners.
- Class sizes are too large.
- Children's interests are subordinated to the rigid promotion of theories and preservation of vested interests.

The solutions generally offered by these submissions were:

- for schools to assess reading problems and progress more effectively;
- to provide teacher training in recognising reading problems;
- to provide earlier funding for reading problems;
- to make schools accountable for their failures;
- to recognise parents' input as valuable;
- to make methods of intervention other than Reading Recovery available.

The need for better systems of assessing reading progress was an aspect of many of these submissions. In its 1997 report on reading (and again in its briefing to the Committee), the ERO identified poorly performing schools' neglect of early and frequent assessment as their major failure. Many parents of failing readers commented on poor quality of assessment. Laypeople though they are, they felt that effective assessment would have alerted them and the schools to their children's difficulties. Many submissions recounted a failure to recognise and/or diagnose the problem early enough for intervention to be swift and effective. Early and accurate assessment is critical. Moreover, the results of the assessment must be communicated to parents early enough for them to take action too.

Another common theme was that reading failure damaged children's self-esteem, with negative implications for their future academic success. Research by Chapman and colleagues[13] bears out what parents instinctively understand:

- After just two years of schooling, the development of very positive or very negative academic self-concepts was strongly predicted by children's letter–name knowledge and understanding of the sounds in spoken words when they started school.
- The reading self-concept of children who were considered to have successfully completed the Reading Recovery programme declined both during and after the programme.
- One-and-a-half years after their completion of Reading Recovery (i.e. at the end of their third year at school), classroom teachers rated children who were 'successful' in Reading Recovery as having more behaviour problems than children who had not been in Reading Recovery. This finding is consistent with research showing that behaviour problems frequently follow from learning problems.[14]

Children's learning experiences have a major effect on their self-concept. This is especially so for learning related self-concept, of academic self-concept. A substantial body of scientific research shows that children who have negative beliefs about themselves as learners eventually lose the motivation to learn and give up trying when they encounter difficult work. They frequently develop a sense of learned helplessness ... . Children who develop initial and ongoing difficulties in learning to read, invariably develop negative academic self-concepts.

J.W. Chapman and W.E. Tunmer, submission to the Select Committee

Other common themes ... with an obvious solution

Politicisation of reading instruction

Submissions from all sectors were critical of the way the issue of reading instruction has been politicised. David Whitehead commented that change will not occur without the political will:

> For too long ideologically driven interest groups have captured reading education in New Zealand. In doing so they have excluded other voices. ... The current English curriculum document is as much a political document reflecting the previous government as an educational document.

In her submission, Gail Cawkwell took a historical view, linking a call for 'back to basics' (part of which is the teaching of phonics) with:

> ... discipline, respect for authority, national allegiance and the 'three Rs'. ... When allegations are made that literacy levels are declining, it is certainly noticeable that these claims are made during times of economic and social uncertainty.

But we don't need arcane explanations for what is starkly evident: a shocking number of children in New Zealand are failing to read. Our focus instead should be on those children. They don't have time to wait for academic debates to be concluded. If children reach the age of nine without becoming competent readers, the opportunity to learn this vital skill is almost closed to them. Doris Ferry, in her submission, expressed her belief that the critical time for phonics instruction is when children are four to six years old.

The system fails Maori in particular

In many submissions, people expressed great concern that the system fails Maori children more than any other group. In 1930 a survey showed that Maori children in native schools had higher average scores in English reading comprehension and maths problem-solving than both Maori and Pakeha children in public schools. This outcome is interpreted as reflecting a strong teaching emphasis on comprehension in English, supported by the number of hours spent on reading.[15] From the beginning of the native school system, some teachers were using children's language and writing texts in Maori. Numerous well-researched examples show too that parent/family/whanau participation is significant to Maori children's learning. There is evidence that low text levels at six years are not inevitable. Similarly there is evidence that expectations about what skills Maori and Pacific Islands children already have on entry to school are considerably lower than their actual level of knowledge and reading ability.

Traditionally and historically Maori learn by rote memory ... [and] have in the past very quickly learned the letter-sound correspondence method of learning to read and write.

Ans Westra, 1963. Alexander Turnbull Library, Wellington M403

I have special feelings for Maori children. I would love to teach Maori four year olds. They need their own culture as all of us need our special culture, but they must learn English literacy to make a satisfactory living with dignity in New Zealand or wherever they choose to go.

Doris Ferry, champion of phonics, submission to the Select Committee

In its submission the NZEI asserted that Maori children are more likely to have just one parent at home, parents with lower levels of formal education, less time devoted to literacy experiences and fewer opportunities to travel widely or to visit museums and libraries. Citing Crooks and Caygill,[16] the NZEI claimed that Maori children may learn to place less value on achievement in individual activities and more on collaborative achievements; for example, they may have more opportunities for gaining peer learning support, learning to relate to larger social groupings and collaborative activities in areas such as music and sport. Early childhood experiences of Maori children were characterised as differing substantially from those of non-Maori, in that they are less likely to attend an early childhood centre and, where they do, many attend kohanga reo with the focus on the development of Maori language skills and cultural experience. Crooks and Caygill argue that these differences may restrict Maori students' opportunities to learn the information and skills that are helpful in schools where English is the medium of instruction.

The NZEI made much of the heartbreaking problems faced by many Maori children who live in poverty. But the reality is that many parents (and children) see schools as a chance to break out of poverty. A more profitable way to look at reading failure and Maori children is to ask, **is there a better way to teach them**? We know that whole language privileges the rich over the poor. Phonics is the democratic way of teaching, a way that can reach every child. You do not need a bookshelf of books to learn phonics. You do not require a rich mum and dad. All you need is a pencil and paper to write the letters of the alphabet, and a teacher who knows how to teach phonics.

Of particular significance here is Chapman and Tunmer's study that showed that, by the middle of the first year of schooling, the gap in reading achievement between Maori and Pakeha children was virtually eliminated – using phonics! In their literacy programmes classroom teachers of new entrant children used special materials and procedures designed to develop children's awareness of sound sequences in spoken words and their ability to use letter–sound patterns in reading unfamiliar words. Not only did the gap between Maori and Pakeha close in year one, but it remained closed to the end of the second year of schooling when the study was concluded. The experimental group achieved an average gain in reading age of 14 months over a comparison group by the end of year two.

Support for the early introduction of phonics for 'at risk' children comes from a recent meta-analysis of studies of how whole language instruction affects the literacy achievement of children from low-income backgrounds.[17] Overall the results indicated that children from poor and minority backgrounds benefited more from a structured ('basal') approach to reading than from whole language instruction, leading the authors to conclude that 'using a whole language approach with low-SES [socioeconomic status] children could widen the gap between advantaged and disadvantaged students'.

Similar results come from a study of the effects of different methods of beginning reading instruction on the reading growth of 'at risk' beginning readers. Foorman and colleagues[18] found that explicitly teaching the alphabetic code and related skills was positively associated with greater improvement in reading. In addition, more explicit instruction in alphabetic coding was more effective than less explicit approaches with children who had lower levels of phonological processing skills at the beginning of the year. A noteworthy finding was that by the end of the year direct instruction in alphabetic coding was closing the gap in reading achievement much more than were less explicit approaches to teaching spelling–sound patterns.

In my book *Zero Tolerance*, I made the point that Maori children from poor homes are not doomed to fail. One way to help them is to take them out of a failing environment. The Targeted Individual Education (TIE) was designed to do that. Under that programme, Maori parents enrolled their children in schools where they could succeed. Evaluation of the TIE programme confirms that children from low-income families can achieve better results when their parents can choose where to send them. Maori students from poor, sometimes dysfunctional backgrounds counted their blessings for having won a scholarship that gave them the opportunity of a lifetime.

Since the abolition of TIE a few years ago, we have lost this opportunity. New Zealand has the widest gap in educational achievement between indigenous and non-indigenous people of any country in the world. I believe that the discrepancy between Maori and non-Maori academic results would disappear within 15 years if the TIE programme were to be reintroduced and extended to child-centred funding for everyone, so that all 'at risk' children can escape the negative consequences of poverty.

Traditionally and historically Maori learn by rote memory. Because we have used whole language teaching, Maori children respond well initially as they can remember the stories and recite whole books. Achievement levels drop off though when more difficult text is encountered. Maoris have in the past very quickly learned the letter–sound correspondence method of learning to read and write. I believe we should raise the level of reading and spelling ability in Maori children by including phonics and word study in our teaching.

Fay Coxon

Many children are now learning to read firstly in Maori and appear to be doing very well. The reasons are unknown but can be assumed to arise from the uncomplicated spelling system and the one to one correspondence of sound and written form.

It would be important to find out whether there is any correlation between learning to read in Maori first and subsequently in English.

Professor Tamati Reedy

Vision and hearing

Finally, some submissions addressed health issues. For example, Rowan Taylor emphasised that improving classroom instruction involves more than a change in teaching practices. To learn effectively, children must be able to see and hear properly. Modern 'child-centred' classrooms are noisy places. Such environments are particularly difficult for students under 13 years of age because they lack the skill to filter out background noise and the vocabulary to fill in the gaps in words and sentences.

A number of children with reading problems also have vision problems that heighten their difficulties. Their problems are often not picked up until it is too late. Often the children themselves do not know they need glasses. A mandatory screening process is needed to check children's visual acuity, as well as their hearing acuity. The old method of reading a chart on the wall is fine for testing whether someone can read signs on the road, but is hopeless for assessing the ability to read a printed word on a page. Today there are many more sophisticated ways of assessing whether a child needs glasses.

Conclusions

In this chapter I have quoted from some of the more than 300 submissions to the Select Committee. Numerous other moving stories were told verbally at the many hearings conducted around the country. Too many children are failing to learn to read. We will reap the consequences in a country where too many citizens lack confidence and are locked out of the information age, the Internet – the future. Parents are often not told that their children have reading problems until it is too late. Those with vested interests in the present system will continue to deny the problems that face this country and say that all is well – when all is not well. Research shows that we have let down a generation of children by not teaching them to read properly. We will never have a happy, successful country until every child (and adult) can read. No one seems to be brave enough to admit they made a mistake and to tackle the problem seriously so that everyone can acquire a skill that is surely a basic human right. Governments in other countries have cut through the vested interests and implemented a more effective phonics-based system of reading instruction. How long do our children have to wait in New Zealand?

Notes

1 Education and Science Select Committee Report on Reading. (2001). *Me panui tatou katoa – Let's all read.* Wellington: New Zealand Parliament.

2 For a discussion of the report of the Literacy Experts Group see: Smith, J.W. (2000). The literacy taskforce in context. In J. Soler & J. Smith (Eds.), *Literacy in New Zealand: Practices, politics and policy since 1900* (pp. 134–143). Auckland: Pearson Education. See also: Nicholson, T. (2002). The social and political contexts of reading: Contemporary literacy policy in Aotearoa New Zealand. In P. Adams & H. Ryan (Eds.), *Learning to read in Aotearoa New Zealand* (pp. 22–50). Palmerston North: Dunmore Press.

3 See also: Nicholson, T., & Gallienne, G. (1995). Struggletown meets Middletown: A survey of reading achievement levels among 13-year-old pupils in two contrasting socio-economic areas. *New Zealand Journal of Educational Studies, 30*, 15–24.
Nicholson, T. (1995). Research note: More news on rich and poor schools, and the news is still not good. *New Zealand Journal of Educational Studies, 30*, 227–228.
Nicholson, T. (1997). Closing the gap on reading failure: Social background, phonemic awareness, and learning to read. In B.A. Blachman (Ed.), *Foundations of reading acquisition and dyslexia: Implications for early intervention* (pp. 381–407). Mahwah, NJ: Lawrence Erlbaum.
Nicholson, T. (1999). Literacy in the family and society. In G.B. Thompson & T. Nicholson (Eds.), *Learning to read: Beyond phonics and whole language* (pp. 1–22). New York: Teachers College Press.
Nicholson, T. (2000). *What makes for a better start in literacy? The results of a 5-year study (a preliminary report).* Paper delivered at a pre-world congress seminar on policy, research and practice, Auckland, New Zealand.

4 See: Moats, L.C. (1999). *Teaching reading **is** rocket science: What expert teachers of reading should know and be able to do.* [Online] American Federation of Teachers <www.aft.org/edissues/downloads/rocketsci.pdf>, accessed 30 May 2002.

5 Tunmer, W.E., Chapman, J.W., Ryan, H., & Prochnow, J.E. (1998). The importance of providing beginning readers with explicit training in phonological processing skills. *Australian Journal of Learning Disabilities, 3*, 4–14.

6 Ministry of Education (1997). *Adult literacy in New Zealand. Results from the international adult literacy survey (1996).* Wellington: Author.

7 Ministry of Education (1997) – see note 6.

8 Taylor, Rowan. (2000). Submission to the Education and Science Select Committee, 352.

9 'Angry Maori mother'. (1980). 'Poor teaching': Letters to the editor. *New Zealand Herald.*

10 Prochnow, J.E., Tunmer, W.E., Chapman, J.W., & Greaney, K.T. (in press). A longitudinal study of early literacy achievement and gender. *New Zealand Journal of Educational Studies.*

11 McNaughton, Stuart. (2000). Submission to the Education and Science Select Committee, 24.

12 Greaney, K. (2001). An investigation of teacher preferences for word identification strategies. *Australian Journal of Language and Literacy, 24*, 23–30.

13 Chapman, J.W., Tunmer, W.E., & Prochnow, J.E. (2001). Does success in the Reading Recovery program depend on developing proficiency in phonological processing skills? A longitudinal study in a whole language instructional context. *Scientific Studies of Reading, 5*, 141–176.

14 Prochnow et al. (in press) – see note 10.

15 McNaughton (2000) – see note 11.

16 Crooks, T., & Caygill, R. (1999). *New Zealand's National Educational Monitoring Project: Maori student achievement, 1995–1998.* Paper presented at the combined annual conference of the New Zealand Association for Research in Education and the Australian Association for Research in Education, Melbourne, Australia.

17 Jeynes, W.H., & Littell, S.W. (2000). A meta-analysis of studies examining the effect of whole language instruction on the literacy of low-SES students. *Elementary School Journal, 101*, 21–33; p. 31.

18 Foorman, B.R., Francis, D.J., Fletcher, J.M., Schatschneider, C., & Mehta, P. (1998). The role of instruction in learning to read: Preventing reading failure in at-risk children. *Journal of Educational Psychology, 90*, 37–55.

CHAPTER 6

The Reading Process – Implications for Teaching Methods

READING IS A PROCESS THAT HAS MANY PARTS TO IT. It involves perceiving the marks on a piece of paper or on a computer screen, recoding them into their phonological forms (words), looking up the meaning of each word in one's mental dictionary, grouping them into phrases and sentences, analysing the meanings of those sentences and, finally, putting together the overall meaning of all the sentences and paragraphs in the text.

The process can be shown in this way:

Reading =
Decoding print ⇨ Accessing word meanings ⇨ Sentence analysis ⇨ Semantic analysis ⇨ meaning

When you think of it this way, reading as a whole is quite simple, even though each part of the process is extremely complicated. Researchers say that if we ever come to understand fully how all these elements work, then we will also understand how the mind works, because reading involves the whole mind. Reading is about visual processing, language processing, thinking, remembering, recalling and problem-solving. Understanding reading is quite a challenge for children and teachers, and even more so for researchers. Through many studies, researchers have developed a range of different views of the reading process.

When our eyes fixate on a word, what happens? This seemingly simple question has proved difficult to answer, provoking much debate among researchers. But we are making progress, especially with the research results that have emerged over the last 20 years. Uncertainties remain, but every year

Reading is a process that has many parts to it and understanding reading is quite a challenge for children, teachers and researchers.

Alexander Turnbull Library, Wellington B-K 546-6

scientists are gaining a better understanding of the ability to read, and to learn to read, with accuracy and understanding.[1]

How do we recognise words?[2]

There are several possible ways of explaining how we recognise words:

- use word shape;
- use context to get meaning;
- identify individual words by processing each letter and following either a direct or an indirect route to the meaning.

The word shape hypothesis

In the 1930s the whole word approach to reading instruction ('look and say') was based on the idea that children could memorise the visual forms of words. One way of memorising is to look at the shape of the word. For example, if we draw a line around *aeroplane*, the word looks like an aeroplane. It was argued that visual cues such as shape, or particular visual features such as the vertical letters in *ladder*, would enable the child to remember the word more easily.

However, this hypothesis has not stood the test of time. If we did read words according to their shape, then it would follow that word identification must be made more difficult by distorting the shapes of words. But Marilyn Adams[3] found evidence against this idea. When presented with words made up of letters of different fonts and sizes, university students could still read them fairly easily. For example, they could read *The cat sat on the mat* just as easily if the word shapes changed to *The cat sat on the MaT*. The students also noticed that when the words were presented to them very quickly, the letters all appeared, in their minds, to be of a similar size and font. Her findings suggested to Adams that readers rapidly transform what they see into more abstract forms of the letters. This process is called the 'ransom note' phenomenon[4] because the text of ransom notes is deliberately disguised, with each word given a unique, odd shape, so we might expect that ransom notes would be hard to read – but they are not.

From their review of other studies that tested the word shape hypothesis, Paap and colleagues[5] concluded that letters quickly change into abstract letter identities early in the word reading process. By this means, skilled readers access their mental lexicons where word meanings are stored. Although they could use word shape to recognise a word, good readers ignore it.

The guessing game (or hypothesis–test) hypothesis

Do we anticipate words by a process of calculated guesswork? If so, then do we need to process all the letters of words? Do we need to sample just some of the visual details of a word in order to confirm each guess? In the 1970s Ken Goodman, founder of the whole language movement, described reading as a 'psycholinguistic' guessing game. He argued the skilled reader only samples the print to confirm predictions about meaning, and does not have to process every letter. 'As the child develops reading skill and speed,' he wrote, 'he uses increasingly fewer graphic cues.'[6] Why would we want to recognise words in this way? Goodman's reasoning was that it takes too long to process all the letters on the page so we take advantage of predictability in English spelling to guess at many of them. It is on this shaky hypothetical ground that whole language is based.

Frank Smith, another early proponent of whole language,[7] argued there is much predictability in the spellings of words. For example, a predictable letter sequence is that *q* is usually followed by *u*. We can also use the predictability of word sequences in sentences (e.g. *ham and* ____) to guess individual letters and meanings, and reduce the amount of visual information we process in reading.

In the 1970s these ideas were attractive to educators, who were concerned that phonics teaching was becoming hopelessly skills-based. Children had to learn hundreds of rules, many with little application. In contrast, the whole language view was saying that learning to read was easy but teachers were making it hard. Its exponents promoted the appealing idea that children will teach themselves to read if given a chance. Frank Smith argued that teachers did not give children enough credit, that children could learn to read words well if they were given meaningful contexts.[8] Teachers started to feel guilty that they were preventing children from learning to read by trying to teach them.

The case against context: eye-movement research

In the 1970s, in the absence of evidence to the contrary, it was difficult to dispute Frank Smith's claims that skilled readers do not read every letter, or even every word or sentence, and that skilled readers read 'meaning', not words. Since the 1970s, however, many studies have cast doubt on the psycholinguistic guessing game hypothesis.

Most convincingly, using sophisticated eye-movement cameras that track exactly what the eyes look at while reading, researchers have shown that the eyes of skilled readers fixate on almost every word on the page.[9] Their eyes process text word by word across each line. Readers may not fixate on every word but, depending on the length of the word, their eyes process nearly every word to some extent.

Whole language supporters claim that children use context to help decode reading books based on the whole language approach. Yet context is a 'fickle' friend, wrong three times out of four.

Pete Little is reproduced with the permission of the author Beverley Randell and the publishers Nelson Thomson Australia Pty Ltd.

Day after day Jonathan said,
"Say this, Pete. Say . . .
I am Pete Little, 10 Hill Road."
Jonathan's Mum and Dad
said it, too.

But Pete did **not** say it.
He said, "Clever Pete."

6

7

This finding overturns earlier whole language ideas that the skilled reader's eyes move around the page 'constructing' the meaning of the text.

Eye-movement studies have also found that context (like *ham and ____*) can reduce the time spent processing a particular word, but only by 10 per cent of the time needed to process each word and then only if the word is highly predictable. A 10 per cent saving in processing time would be useful if every word was highly predictable but most words are not. Context cues help only about 25 per cent of the time.[10] We do not skip words, except when they occur extremely frequently, like *the*. We do not skip sentences in normal reading. The eye plods along each line rather boringly, reading every word in sequence.

New Zealand whole language proponents such as John Smith and Warwick Elley[11] have counter-argued that when we are fixating on a word, how does anyone know what we are doing? We might be sampling letters or looking at the general shapes of words. But eye-movement researchers have found that skilled readers seem to be processing words in a very detailed way. They notice even slight misspellings.[12] Such findings suggest that words are processed at the letter level.

We cannot process a whole sentence at one time because our eyes have a limited range of acuity, which allows us to process about six letters at once. That is, when we look at a page, we do not see the whole page or even a whole sentence; all we see clearly is about six letter spaces. If the reader is processing a lot of short words, then it might not be necessary to fixate on every word, as the reader could process letters in the next word along while looking at the word before it. From our own experience of reading, we might feel that our eyes are moving constantly, not stopping to look at every word. But they hardly move at all. They spend 95 per cent of the time quite still, processing letters in words.

Good readers are skilled at word recognition, so skilled that there is little opportunity for context to help out. Context, a 'fickle friend', is wrong three times out of four. As we have seen in chapter 3, poor readers rely heavily on context, combining it with partial decoding skill. Their strategy puts them at a disadvantage because it is less efficient than the ability to recognise words without relying on context. Researchers nowadays know that it is the poor reader and not the good reader who relies on context cues to read words. However, their findings have taken a long time to make an impact on the classroom and it is still not clear that the average teacher in a New Zealand whole language classroom knows about them.

What happens when the reader comes across a word that is ambiguous, such as *bat* in the sentence *The bat is in the attic*? It is in this area of word and sentence meaning that context does most of its work, rather than in recognition of words. When this kind of ambiguity occurs, the reader seems to hold off making a decision about the meaning until it becomes clear. The uncertainty does not last long, because the reader soon uses context to resolve the problem.

It seems that when reading normally, skilled readers do not guess ahead. They decode words at the letter level very early during the fixation of a word and resolve word ambiguities and meanings before moving to the next word fixation. Researchers have used the term **immediacy hypothesis** to describe these linguistic decisions that are made during each brief fixation.[13]

Letter processing hypotheses

So how do we recognise printed words? If we don't rely on word shape or context, the only other distinguishing characteristics of a word are its letters. So how do readers use these letters? Do they identify all the letters as a complete pattern? Do they process the letters in chunks of two or three at a time? Or do they identify the first letter followed by the next letter, and so on?

Researchers are still working on these questions. However, most researchers agree that all the letters in each word do get processed. What is not clear is how we go from the print on the page or computer screen to the words in our mental lexicon. Do we take the 'direct route' to meaning of looking printed words up directly by their letters, which we have stored in memory? Or do we take the 'indirect route' of recoding letters into phonemes and look up the word in its phonological form in memory?

The **direct access hypothesis** is that we go straight from letters to meaning when we identify words, without recoding letters into sound first. An early version of this hypothesis was that skilled readers have identified the alphabetic forms of many millions of words through reading and have remembered them, so all they have to do is match the printed forms with the same visual forms in memory. Most researchers nowadays think storing words only in visual form would present an impossible memory task to a reader of English. In a language like Chinese, many words have to be remembered at least to some extent visually. In English, the memory task would be equivalent to memorising 50,000 telephone numbers.[14]

However, a modern version of the hypothesis shows that direct access is possible in other ways. The ability to use phonics enables a child to associate letter patterns in words with their spoken forms. By applying phonics, the child builds up a store of sight words that act as mnemonics or memory aids in recognising the visual form of a word. The connection of the visual form to its sound representation provides a strong way of remembering words, so that the written form of a word immediately evokes the spoken form in memory.[15] The reader may need only to sound out a word a few times before it is well established as a visual-phonological entry in the reader's mental dictionary.

It seems probable that only very frequent words like *the* might be stored totally visually. Although the question is still under debate, it seems that all other words will be stored in a way that evokes sight and sound at the same time during reading.

Nevertheless, it appears that the direct access hypothesis does not give a complete explanation. Accessing words 'directly' is something the skilled reader can do, but not the beginner. The child must learn first to recode words according to their phonemes. That is, the child must be able to sound out words. So at least initially the reader must access the mental lexicon indirectly.

The **indirect access** hypothesis, therefore, is that we recode letters into systematic phonemes when we identify a word. We then search for the word in our mental dictionary, looking for its phonemic representation. For example, we convert *health* into systematic phonemes (e.g. /h-ea-l/ + /th/). We then access the meaning of the word just as if it had been spoken to us.[16]

There is evidence both for and against this hypothesis.[17] The most interesting evidence that supports it is that readers are more likely to miss a spelling error if it 'sounds' like the correct word (e.g. *werk* instead of *work*). When people are asked to count the number of times the letter *f* occurs in *finished files are the result of years of scientific study*, most count only four instances instead of six. They miss the *f* in *of*, which occurs twice, because in these two instances the letter **sounds like** a *v*, not an *f*. People also find it confusing when you ask them to answer a question like *Is a rows a flower?* because *rows* **sounds like** *rose*, making it more difficult to say that the statement is false.

A more practical argument in favour of the indirect route to meaning is that it is hard to find another way to explain how we learn to read. We know that beginner readers try to avoid sounding out words by remembering visual features (e.g. the 'tail' on *dog*), but this strategy breaks down quickly and must be replaced by 'sounding out'.[18]

A third possibility for word recognition is that skilled readers use **both access routes** – that is, both direct visual and indirect phonological routes – to the mental lexicon. According to the dual-route hypothesis or horse-race model, reading words is like a horse race, with a race for the lexicon along both routes. Alternatively, in the co-operative or connectionist model, both routes work together to find the word.[19]

Although the debate about how we recognise words continues, it is clear that phonological recoding is a major part of how we recognise words. Reading words is not a guessing game.

Implications for teaching

In our efforts to work out how best to teach children to read, we can take three important concepts from the research findings on word recognition:

1. Good readers ignore word shape and quickly change the letters of words into abstract letter units early in the word reading process.
2. The importance of context lies in its help with word and sentence meaning rather than in recognition of words.
3. Readers process all the letters in nearly all words.

In New Zealand, whole language proponents disagree with these ideas. Rather than process every letter, they say, the skilled reader 'samples' some of the letters or looks at the shape of the word. Elley and Smith, for example, claimed that readers 'respond to the letters they see, especially at the beginning and end of each word; they respond to the shape of the word, common suffixes and other recurring spelling patterns'.[20] The evidence recounted in this chapter presents a strong case against such claims, with significant implications for how reading instruction should be changed in this country. The following research findings contain further implications for teaching practice.

Teach spelling patterns

As Adams has noted,[21] the great value of vowels is that they signal the presence of syllables in words. To break words into syllables, the reader must know that a syllable has a vowel sound at its core.

[Teaching practice in New Zealand takes the child from segments] of meaningful text, to words, and then letters rather than the reverse. ... When New Zealand children are taught new letter sound links or common blends this is usually done in the context of a sentence or story.

Smith and Elley[22]

[O]verreliance on contextual clues should be a source of concern for the educator rather than a source of pride, for it is a strong sign that the reader's orthographic knowledge and skills have not been properly developed.

Marilyn Adams[23]

Good readers are able to break long words quickly into syllables and other useful chunks. In contrast, poor readers are less aware of syllable structure in long words and thus have trouble reading them.

To make progress, the poor reader must learn to break words into syllables (e.g. *rab-bit*, *kan-ga-roo*, *sal-a-man-der*, *con-sis-tent-ly*) and then analyse individual syllables in terms of letter blends (e.g. *cr-*, *bl-*), digraphs (e.g. *ch*, *sh*) and phonogram patterns (e.g. *-ill*, *-at*, *-up*).

Help poor readers automatise their reading and spelling

Poor readers are often slow and inaccurate in their reading, in contrast to the speed of skilled readers. One way to improve the approach of poor readers is to automatise their reading and spelling of the most frequent words in their text materials. The 100 most frequent words in text make up more than half of the words a child reads. If the child can read these words effortlessly, then he or she can devote more mental energy to working out more important words. There are only a small number of highly frequent words, but many are not spelled regularly and must be learned by practising them again and again so that they can be read effortlessly.[24]

Find better ways of teaching phonemic awareness

Poor readers are often unable to recode words phonologically. The stumbling block is a lack of phonemic awareness.

Researchers have examined ways to teach phonemic awareness. The Russian researcher Elkonin, for example, found that children in kindergarten and first grade were able to learn how to analyse sounds in words in 10 to 12 lessons by learning to segment spoken words.[25] The child named a picture, then said the word sound by sound and at the same time put down a cardboard chip (different colour for consonants and vowels) for each sound. For example, a child could be taught to put down a token for each of the four phonemes in the spoken word *stop*:

/s/ /t/ /ɔ/ /p/

Phonemic awareness is usually taught verbally, without using letters of the alphabet. The focus is on teaching children to 'hear' sounds in words, not to relate sounds to letters.

In England, Bryant and colleagues[26] found that children's knowledge of traditional English nursery rhymes at three years of age strongly predicted their reading ability at six years of age. It seems that learning nursery rhymes at an early age makes children more sensitive to the phonology of words.

A difficulty with training of the first phoneme is the concept of 'beginning sound'. Phil Gough (personal communication) has suggested using I Spy games to teach preschoolers about beginning sounds. For example, 'I spy with my little eye something beginning with the sound /f/' would be said using the first phoneme of the word, rather than the letter name of the thing that is spied.

New Zealand research suggests that the following activities are helpful:[27]

- At the preschool level, engage children in activities that direct their attention to the sounds in words, such as clapping the syllables in words, as well as rhyming and alliteration games.
- Teach students to segment and blend. One approach is to ask children to find a certain object in a box of different objects where you say the word slowly, phoneme by phoneme. For example, instead of asking them to find the *rabbit* in the box, you ask them to find the *r-a-bb-i-t*. In this activity you are segmenting the phonemes, and a child has to put the phonemes back together in his or her mind, figure out what word you are saying, and then take it out of the box.
- Combine training in segmentation and blending with instruction in letter–sound relationships. That is, once children are familiar with phoneme blending and segmenting, use letters to represent the phonemes. For example, in the Elkonin technique, the next step after phoneme awareness training is to use letters instead of chips:

S	T	O	P

Here are some other recommendations for phonemic awareness activities:[28]

- Keep a sense of playfulness and fun. Avoid drill and rote memorisation.
- Use group settings that encourage interaction among children.
- Encourage children's curiosity about language and their experimentation with it.
- Allow for and be prepared for individual differences.
- Make sure the tone of the activity is fun and informal, rather than evaluative.
- Spend a few minutes each day engaging preschool and year one children in oral activities that emphasise the sounds of language.

Examples of phonemic awareness tasks

Note: do not use letters for these tasks.[30]

1. *Rhyme: Does* fish *rhyme with* dish*?*
2. *Phoneme recognition: Does* fish *start with the* f *sound? Does wash end with the* sh *sound?*
3. *Blending phonemes: What word is this?* f-i-sh
4. *Identification of first, middle or final sound: What is the first sound in* fish*?*
5. *Odd one out: What word starts with a different sound?* star, cat, sock
6. *Phoneme segmentation (i.e. isolating the sounds of a word in correct sequence): What are the three sounds in* fish*?*
7. *Phoneme segmentation by counting: How many sounds are there in the word* fish*?*
8. *Deleting phonemes: Say* fish*. Now say* fish *without the* f (-ish)*.*
9. *Deleting and isolating the phoneme: Say* cat*. Now say* at *. What sound did I leave out?*
10. *Phoneme substitution: Say* meet*. Now say it with* f *instead of* m.

Overseas support for reading instruction based on phonics and phonemic awareness

Overseas experts have reached similar conclusions about what the research evidence on word recognition and skilled reading means for reading instruction. For example, Dr Bonnie Macmillan, Research Fellow at the Institute of Economic Affairs, London,[29] concluded from the evidence that successful reading programmes:

> *There is little correlation between developmental stages and phonemic awareness. Every school child is ready for some phonemic instruction. In fact, if the children who fall behind do not begin receiving explicit teacher-initiated instruction, they are very likely to continue falling further and further behind. Phonemic awareness and other important reading skills are learned and do not develop naturally.*
>
> ***Keith Stanovich*[31]**

- focus primarily on teaching the skills that matter most to subsequent reading achievement;
- concentrate early on teaching letter–sound associations rather than teaching alphabet knowledge incidentally;
- teach both phoneme and letter–sound skills together, rather than focusing on just one of these components at a time.

She also found that reading instruction that produced better readers focused on:

- teaching individual phonemes early;
- teaching phonemic awareness and letter–sound skills in isolation from text at the beginning stages, instead of taking text-based approaches such as shared reading.

In the United States, the National Reading Panel[32] reported that a combination of teaching phonics and word sounds and giving feedback on oral reading was the most effective way to teach. The favoured approach included:

- teaching children to break apart and manipulate the sounds in words (phonemic awareness);
- teaching them that these sounds are represented by letters of the alphabet that can be blended together to form words (phonics);
- having them practise what they learned by reading aloud with guidance and feedback (guided oral reading);
- applying reading comprehension strategies to guide and improve reading comprehension.

Also in the United States and based on research evidence, the National Institute for Child Health and Development (NICHD) emphasises developing phonemic awareness early.[33] To prevent reading problems, classroom teachers should incorporate the following elements into their reading programmes:[34]

- Begin teaching **phonemic awareness directly at an early age**, before children begin formal schooling. Preschool teachers should teach phonemic awareness, the alphabet and simple letter–sound relationships.
- Teach each **sound–spelling correspondence explicitly**. In regard to the 'balanced instruction' that whole language proponents call for, a common misconception is that the teacher should teach sound–spelling relationships in the context of real stories. Yet this kind of instruction is less effective than explicit instruction.[35] In explicit instruction, the teacher says the phoneme to the child, for example, 'This letter says *mmmmm*', rather than just conveying it indirectly, as in 'The word *mat* starts with *mmmm*'. Children learn more easily if they are told the phoneme explicitly.
- Teach **frequent, highly regular sound–spelling relationships systematically**. Many of the most frequent words in English have regular spellings with specific letter–sound correspondence

rules (e.g. *cap, sad, get, card, chat*). The most effective instructional programmes teach children to read successfully with only 40 to 50 sound–spelling relationships. (See appendix 1 for some examples of how to teach these correspondences.)

- Show children **exactly how to sound out words**. After children have learned two or three sound–spelling correspondences (e.g. *m, s, a*), begin teaching them how to blend the sounds into words (e.g. *am, Sam*). Show them how to move sequentially from left to right through spellings as they 'sound out' or say the sound for each spelling.
- Use **connected, decodable text** for children to practise the sound–spelling relationships they learn. The findings of the NICHD research emphasise that children need extensive practice in applying their phonics knowledge to reading. To get this practice, they need decodable text. A beginner book like *Hop on Pop* by Dr Seuss is a good example of easy, decodable text.

  Some reading programmes teach add-on phonics rules but they do not match what children read in texts. For example, in one meaning-based reading programme that included an add-on phonics component, the first sentence was: *The dog is up*. Yet the only letter–sound relationships the children had learned up to this point were: *d, m, s, r*, and *t*. By applying what they had learned in the phonics component, the children could read this much of the sentence: —- *d*— —. That is, it was impossible for the children to use their phonics knowledge to read.[36]
- Use **interesting stories to develop language comprehension**. The NICHD research ruled out use of stories as reading material for non-readers, but not use of interesting authentic stories altogether. Any connected text that is graded either for decoding difficulty or for vocabulary difficulty cannot provide entire coherent stories in the early stages of reading acquisition. During this early stage of reading acquisition, children can still benefit from authentic stories because the teacher can read such stories to them.
- Teach **comprehension separately**. It does not just happen on its own. Comprehension instruction is distinct from decoding instruction while children are learning to decode. Dymock and Nicholson[37] have shown how comprehension instruction can be taught separately from decoding, even for the simplest beginner texts.

  During the early stages of reading acquisition, children's oral language comprehension level is much higher than their reading comprehension level. The material used to build their decoding skills should be geared towards this purpose, with attention to meaning. Comprehension strategies and new vocabulary should be taught using orally presented stories and texts that are more sophisticated than the early decodable text the children read.

What teachers need to know about teaching phonics[38]

To teach phonics well, the teacher needs to understand the phonological structure of language. However, many teachers do not have an explicit understanding of how language works. They may understand rhyme, syllables, morphemes and so on implicitly, yet struggle to explain them. Wide gaps in the language knowledge of education students, who were also experienced teachers, were evident in a study by Louisa Moats in the United States.[39] In a replication of the Moats study, Tom Nicholson[40] found the same lack of understanding with New Zealand teacher trainees. In a test situation, responding to a question on how they would recognise a word of Greek origin, for example, one student wrote, 'It will be wearing a toga'.

Such research findings show how important it is for our teachers to increase their understanding of the phonological structure of the language we speak. Louisa Moats, who has written widely on how to teach language awareness knowledge to teachers, has proposed the following as key points for teachers to understand clearly.[41]

On **phonological awareness**

- Phonological awareness normally develops over a number of years, progressing from early rhyming abilities to explicit awareness of the individual phonemes.
- It is distinct from both phonics and the ability to read and spell. A young pre-reader with no letter knowledge may nonetheless be able to perform a variety of listening activities such as rhyming, tapping out the number of syllables in a word, or listing words that begin with a certain sound.
- To be a skilled reader, it is necessary to realise that words are comprised of individual speech sounds that are more or less represented by letters. Without this knowledge, the learner finds the English writing system an enigma.

On the **morphemic structure** of words

- Morphemes are the smallest meaningful units in words. They may be whole words (e.g. *foot*, *finger*) or parts of words (e.g. *un+teach+able*, *medic+al*).
- Appreciation of morphemes is a second area of structural awareness for the beginning or poor reader/speller.
- Awareness of the morphemes in words facilitates both reading and spelling, and not only for the advanced reader. For example, beginning writers often spell plurals and past tense forms as they sound (e.g. *dogz*, *wakt*) before they grasp the concept that plural is represented by the consistent spelling *-s* or that past tense is represented by the consistent spelling *-ed*.

- To progress to more advanced stages of reading and spelling, the learner needs to realise that the spelling of meaningful word parts often stays constant even when pronunciation changes from one word form to another, as in *compete* and *competition*, *resign* and *resignation*, *define* and *definition*.

On **code-emphasis** instruction

- The importance of code-emphasis instruction for students who do not automatically learn to read and spell is a key finding in reading research.
- The inclusion of code-based instruction is not necessarily the 'phonics' of old that was largely workbook-oriented.
- When it is skilfully implemented, systematic code instruction is most effective for beginning and for problem readers.

Conclusions

Trends in reading come and go. If a new idea is appealing enough, like the idea that we read words by their shape or the idea that we mostly guess what words are without looking at the letters, it seems to take on a life of its own and it is difficult to stop it from becoming established in mainstream thinking. This momentum encouraged the establishment of the look and say approach in the mid 20th century, so that reading instruction focused on the 'shapes' of words. Later in the same century it also assisted the whole language approach, which argued reading is only incidentally visual, to become established as mainstream classroom practice.

It has taken decades of scientific research to show that these ideas were wrong, and teaching practice often lags many years behind research. Trends in reading also often build up a protective wall of stakeholders who do not want to concede that their ideas have turned out to be wrong. These barriers are evident in New Zealand today, where the Ministry of Education, the primary teachers' union, and some university and college of education lecturers are defending the whole language approach, even though there is a huge weight of research evidence against whole language theory.

The country has to decide which side is right: the academics who have done the research that has cast doubt on whole language claims or those who defend the status quo, even though the status quo is producing a long tail of children who are not learning to read. The status quo is also discriminating against those children who are not phonologically ready to learn to read, especially those from poor homes and from Maori homes. England and the United States, among others, have taken the hard decision and insisted that schools teach phonics seriously. Why can't we do the same?

Notes

1 Stanovich, K.E. (2000). *Progress in understanding reading: Scientific foundations and new frontiers*. New York: Guilford Press.
Thompson, G.B., Tunmer, W.E., & Nicholson, T. (1994). *Reading acquisition processes*. Clevedon, England: Multilingual Matters.
Underwood, G., & Batt, V. (1996). *Reading and understanding*. Oxford: Blackwell.

2 For a longer summary, see: Nicholson, T. (2000). *Reading the writing on the wall: Debates, challenges and opportunities in the teaching of reading*. Palmerston North: Dunmore Press.

3 Adams, M.J. (1990). *Beginning to read*. Cambridge, MA: MIT Press.

4 Gough, P.B. (1984). Word recognition. In P.D. Pearson, R. Barr, M.L. Kamil, & P. Rosenthal (Eds.), *Handbook of reading research* (Vol. 1, pp. 225–253). White Plains, NY: Longman.

5 Paap, K.R., Newsome, S.L., & Noel, R.W. (1984). Word shape's in poor shape for the race to the lexicon. *Journal of Experimental Psychology, 10*, 413–428.

6 Goodman, K.S. (1970). Reading: A psycholinguistic guessing game. In H. Singer & R.B. Ruddell (Eds.), *Theoretical models and processes of reading* (Vol. 1, pp. 259–271). Newark, DE: International Reading Association; p. 266.

7 Smith, F. (1971). *Understanding reading*. New York: Holt, Rinehart & Winston.

8 Rose, S. (Producer). (1975). *How do you read?* [Television Documentary]. London: BBC Horizon.

9 Rayner, K., & Pollatsek, A. (1989). *The psychology of reading*. Hillsdale, NJ: Erlbaum.

10 Gough, P.B. (1983). Context, form and interaction. In K. Rayner (Ed.), *Eye movements in reading: Perceptual and language processes* (pp. 203–211). San Diego, CA: Academic Press.
Hill, D., & Nicholson, T. (1985). Good readers don't guess: Taking another look at the issue of whether children read words better in context or in isolation. *Reading Psychology, 6*, 181–198.
Nicholson, T., Pearson, P.D., & Dykstra, R. (1979) Effects of embedded errors and oral reading anomalies on children's understanding of stories. *Journal of Reading Behavior, 11*, 339–354.

11 Smith, J.W., & Elley, W.B. (1994). *Learning to read in New Zealand*. Auckland: Longman Paul.

12 Rayner & Pollatsek (1989) – see note 9. Adams (1990) – see note 3.

13 Just, M.A., & Carpenter, P.A. (1987). *The psychology of reading and language comprehension*. Newton, MA: Allyn & Bacon.

14 Adams, M.J., & Bruck, M. (1993). Word recognition: The interface of educational policies and scientific research. *Reading and Writing: An Interdisciplinary Journal, 5*, 113–139.

15 Ehri, L.C. (1992). Reconceptualising the development of sight word reading and its relationship to decoding. In P.B. Gough, L.C. Ehri, & R. Treiman (Eds.), *Reading acquisition* (pp. 107–143). Hillsdale, NJ: Erlbaum.
Thompson, G.B. (1999). The processes of learning to identify words. In G.B. Thompson & T. Nicholson (Eds.), *Learning to read: Beyond phonics and whole language*. New York: Teachers College Press.

16 Foss, D., & Hakes, D. (1978). *Psycholinguistics*. Hillsdale, NJ: Prentice Hall.

17 Gough (1984) – see note 4.

18 For a review, see: Tunmer, W.E., & Chapman, J.W. Theoretical contexts of reading: How children learn to read (and why some don't). In P. Adams & H. Ryan, (Eds.), *Learning to read in Aotearoa New Zealand* (pp. 61–64). Palmerston North: Dunmore Press.
See also: Nicholson, T. (2000). *Reading the writing on the wall: Debates, challenges and opportunities in the teaching of reading*. Palmerston North: Dunmore Press; chapter 7.

19 Rayner & Pollatsek (1989) – see note 9. Adams (1990) – see note 3.

20 Smith & Elley (1994); p. 78 – see note 11.

21 Adams (1990) – see note 3.

22 Smith & Elley (1994); p. 140 – see note 11.

23 Adams (1990) – see note 3.

24 Nicholson, T. (1998). The flashcard strikes back. *The Reading Teacher, 52*, 188–192.
Tan, A., & Nicholson, T. (1997). Flashcards revisited: Training poor readers to read words faster improves their comprehension of text. *Journal of Educational Psychology, 89*, 276–288.

25 Elkonin, D.B. (1973). USSR. In J. Downing (Ed.), *Comparative reading*. (pp. 551–580). New York: Macmillan.

26 Bryant, P., Bradley, L., Maclean, M, & Crossland, J. (1989). Nursery rhymes, phonological skills and reading. *Journal of Child Language, 16*, 407–428.

27 Castle, J. (1999). Learning and teaching phonological awareness. In G.B. Thompson & T. Nicholson. (Eds.), *Learning to read: Beyond phonics and whole language* (pp. 55–73). New York: Teachers College Press.
For the 'box of objects' activity, see: Grace, C. (2002). *Teaching phonemic awareness and learning to read*. Unpublished Master's thesis, University of Auckland, Auckland.
For a review of phonemic awareness activities, see: Nicholson, T. (1999). *At the cutting edge: Recent research on learning to read and spell*. Wellington: New Zealand Council for Educational Research.

28 Yopp, H.K. (1992). Developing phonemic awareness in young children. *The Reading Teacher, 45*, 696–703.

29 Cited by Taylor, Rowan. (2000). Submission to the Education and Science Select Committee, 352.

30 Castle (1999) – see note 27.
Lewkowicz, N.K. (1980). Phonemic awareness training: What to teach and how to teach it. *Journal of Educational Psychology*, 72, 686–700.

31 Stanovich, K.E. (1994). Romance and reality. *The Reading Teacher*, *47*, 280–291.

32 Ehri, L.C., Nunes, S.R., Willow, D.M., Schuster, B.V., Yaghoub-Zadeh, Z., & Shanahan, T. (2001). Phonemic awareness instruction helps children learn to read: Evidence from the National Reading Panel's meta-analysis. *Reading Research Quarterly*, *36*, 250–287.

33 Lyon, Reid. (1999). *Education research: Is what we don't know hurting our children?* [Online] National Institute for Child Health and Development <www.nichd.nih.gov/about/crmc/cdb/r_house.htm> accessed 30 May 2002.

34 A review of NICHD research mentions these activities: Grossen, B. (1997, November). *A synthesis of research on reading from the National Institute of Child Health and Human Development.* Unpublished manuscript, University of Oregon.

35 Foorman, B.R., Francis, D.J., Fletcher, J.M., Schatsneider, C., & Mehta, P. (1998). The role of instruction in learning to read: Preventing reading failure in at-risk children. *Journal of Educational Psychology*, *90*, 1–15.

36 Grossen (1997) – see note 34.

37 Dymock, S.J., & Nicholson, T. (1999). *Reading comprehension: What is it? How do you teach it?* Wellington: New Zealand Council for Educational Research.
See also supplementary materials: Dymock, S.J., & Nicholson, T. (2001). *Reading comprehension supplementary materials: Narrative.* Wellington: New Zealand Council for Educational Research.
Dymock, S.J., & Nicholson, T. (2002). *Reading comprehension supplementary materials: Transactional.* Wellington: New Zealand Council for Educational Research.

38 Phonics is discussed in: Nicholson (2000) – see note 2.

39 Moats, L.C. (1995). The missing foundation in teacher education. *American Educator*, *19*, 9, 43–52.

40 Nicholson, T. (1999, November). *'How many sounds in ox?' A survey of the linguistic knowledge of teacher education trainees.* Paper presented at New Zealand Linguistics Conference, Palmerston North, New Zealand.

41 Moats, L.C. (1995). The missing foundation in teacher education. *American Educator*, *19*, 43–51.
See also: Moats, L.C. (1999). *Teaching reading **is** rocket science: What expert teachers of reading should know and be able to do.* [Online] American Federation of Teachers <www.aft.org/edissues/downloads/rocketsci.pdf>, accessed 30 May 2002.
Moats, L.C. (2000). *Speech to print: Language essentials for teachers.* Baltimore, MD: Paul H. Brookes.

CHAPTER 7

Towards a Literate Future – Teacher Training and Government Strategies

LEARNING TO READ IS DIFFICULT FOR MANY PEOPLE. The debate over reading instruction wouldn't exist if teaching children to read was as simple as providing the assistance of an enthusiastic but untrained tutor. The irregularity of some English spelling patterns makes the task even more difficult. To understand fully what they are demanding of their pupils, teachers must have a good understanding of the reading process.

Although data on how reading is taught in New Zealand schools are scarce, it is clear that reading instruction has moved away from phonics towards whole language.[1] Since the 1970s a whole generation of teachers has been taught the whole language approach to reading. Very few of today's teachers know anything about phonics because they did not learn how to teach phonics during their teacher training.

For many years teacher training programmes have followed the English curriculum in their approach to teaching about reading. Whole language principles are strongly embedded in the present English curriculum. For example, at levels one and two, which are the early stages of reading, the Ministry of Education curriculum document[2] states that 'students are encouraged to sample and predict, make approximations, and use cue sources to cross-check and confirm their understanding'. This is pure whole language talk, in that the child is taught to predict and guess at words rather than decode them according to their letters.

Several New Zealand studies suggest that New Zealand teachers, in the main, do follow the whole language principles of the English curriculum. In a survey of 16 primary school teachers, for example, Greaney[3] asked which instructional prompts they would use to help a child work out a difficult word.

In a submission to the Parliamentary Education and Science Select Committee, a University of Waikato lecturer stated that he was not aware of any research on how New Zealand teachers teach reading. According to him, most analysis is based merely on the past and present official syllabi – documents that are 'official' guides. But it is not known whether teachers have followed their guidance or, if they have, how they have followed it.

Recipes for Happy Children.
Given some trees,
Some grass and some water,
You'll have no Trouble
With your son or your daughter.
We play in the gardens
We swim in the Sea
We swing in the parks
And we like being free
We seldom say 'don't'
And we never say 'won't'
Although 'mother's as busy
as she can be.

Three out of four teachers preferred to use context cues, such as 'read to the end of the sentence', rather than phonics cues such as 'sound it out'.

Among a random sample of 92 teachers from 20 primary schools in Auckland, there was a high response rate to Hughes' questionnaire designed to identify the approach that teachers followed.[4] Teachers' views of reading were highly consistent with the whole language approach. For example, when asked to write about the advantages of whole language, teachers listed many points, such as the love of reading, opportunity to read quality children's books, and reading for meaning. They listed correspondingly few disadvantages of whole language. When asked the same questions in regard to phonics, however, teachers were able to list many disadvantages, such as boring worksheets, repetitive drill and irregular spellings of words, but few advantages.

In another study of 25 teachers, Nicholson and Lam[5] gave three hypothetical scenarios: one where a child had made reading errors that reflected use of a whole language strategy, one where the child used a look and say strategy, and one where the child used phonics strategies to sound out words. They found that teachers preferred the whole language scenario, and rejected both the look and say and the phonics scenarios. When asked to describe the reading process, many teachers responded in ways that reflected the whole language approach.

Thus the available evidence indicates that most New Zealand teachers teach whole language strategies for reading. This tendency is not surprising because it is what they are trained to do in their years of teacher preparation and because it is the approach required in the English curriculum. In the Hughes study, the finding that teachers could list many disadvantages of phonics, but few advantages, suggests that they are not taught the positive side of phonics instruction during their own training. Their inability to list advantages for phonics also indicates that they are not using this method of teaching in their classrooms.

Ironically, whole language strategies are not what good readers prefer to use to work out difficult words. They prefer phonics strategies. In a survey of 152 children in years one and two in 22 schools, Tunmer and colleagues[6] asked each child, 'When you are reading on your own and come across a word that you don't know, what do you do to try and figure out what the word is?' At both year levels the majority of children said they used word-level information – that is, the letters in words – rather than guessing. More importantly, the children in year one who preferred word-level information were more likely to make good progress in learning to read in years two and three. In addition, children who later received Reading Recovery tuition were four times more likely to have said in their first year of school that they preferred using whole language strategies such as guessing at the words.

A retired teacher educated from 1928-1935 is thankful to have been taught to read by sounding the letters from first day at school.

Alexander Turnbull Library, Wellington. 37095½

I was educated in a country school in the years 1928–1935. ... From my first day at school I was taught to read by sounding the letters. The only thing that matches that for me today is doing a cryptic crossword. For instance one of today's clues in The Press was: a biting ditch insect (9 letters). The answer was: trenchant – just a matter of putting the parts together to make the whole, isn't it?

A retired teacher[10]

Further evidence in support of the importance of phonological recoding skills for New Zealand children comes from an Auckland study by Castle and colleagues.[7] They taught a group of children phonemic awareness and simple phonics skills. The trained children made significant gains in phonemic awareness, reading and spelling skills compared with two control groups. Moreover, when followed up a year later, only 23 per cent of the trained group (out of a total of 17 children) required Reading Recovery compared with 43 per cent of the control group (out of a total of 32 children).

How well trained are teachers to teach reading?

The reports of the Literacy Taskforce[8] and the Literacy Experts Group,[9] along with the submissions from the Education Review Office to the Parliamentary Education and Science Select Committee, only hint at answers to the question of just how well trained to teach reading our teachers are. Although they constantly stress the need for the best possible teaching to be available to children, all these groups give little detail of how to go about it. No doubt they are scared off by the prospect of an outcry from the teacher education institutions if they were to dare set out guidelines for teachers. Support for the best possible teaching of all children is one of the planks of the government's literacy and numeracy strategy but it is not clear what this principle means in practical terms to teacher training.

The Literacy Taskforce recommended that a statement of best practice in teaching be drawn up and sent to schools. Although shying away from saying what the statement should cover, the members stated that teachers needed to emphasise developing word-level skills and strategies with struggling readers. All teachers must be skilled with a wide range of strategies so that they can draw on the one that is best for a particular child's needs instead of trying to balance approaches or slavishly following a particular approach for political reasons.

Doubt regarding the adequacy of current teacher training, either at preservice level or for ongoing teacher education, is reflected in recommendation 15 of the Literacy Experts Group report. It advised:

> Good practitioners:
> Reflect on both practice and theoretical knowledge and apply this to their literacy programmes.
> Have access to and learn from ongoing professional development, as theoretical ideas and concepts of best practice change over time.
> Can explain the purposes and justify the approaches used in literacy instruction.

Yet the Literacy Experts Group admitted that they did not know, first, what comprised current literacy training in preservice teacher education or, second, what was the longer-term effectiveness of teacher education with regard to literacy instruction. Without this evidence, how can we say to what extent teacher education providers are doing an adequate job of providing trainees with both content and pedagogical skills to effectively teach young children to read?

For its part, the ERO made a diplomatic submission to the Education and Science Select Committee but at the same time it hit straight at the heart of the problem with teacher training in this area. The ERO found that few teachers in the schools it studied really understood the concept of phonological awareness. Teachers lacked a structured means of assessing phonological awareness, which meant there was a significant shortfall in the information available to them when they had to assess this vital ability in their learners.

When teachers were asked to talk about the assessment of children's phonological awareness many went directly to knowledge of the alphabet. None of the teachers talked about a way of assessing children's phonological awareness.

ERO, submission to the Select Committee

Research shows clearly that learning to read and spell requires awareness that words are built of 'sounds' (i.e. phonemes) and that methods of teaching reading need to ensure that learners develop this awareness. Are teachers ready to implement phonemic awareness instruction? The available evidence discussed above indicates they are not in New Zealand. Similarly, Rath,[11] who surveyed 121 classroom teachers, specialist reading teachers and teacher trainees in the United States, found that many had difficulty in understanding what 'phonemes' were. Many teachers surveyed were also unclear about the difference between phonemic awareness and phonics.

Assessing phonological awareness, however, is not difficult. Instruments to test for a child's phonemic awareness tend to be short, easy to administer, reliable and valid. Yopp,[12] for example, provides quick (seven-minute) and easy-to-administer phonological awareness tests. In New Zealand, Nicholson's book[13] on phonemic awareness and phonics includes the Gough-Kastler-Roper test of phonemic awareness, a short 10-minute test that has good reliabilities and has been field-tested successfully on hundreds of children.

How can we prepare teachers better?

To find out what teachers must know to be effective in teaching reading to 95 per cent of their pupils (the proportion that we know **can** learn to read), we need to consider what recent research has revealed about the reading process. Then we need to figure out what the implications of these findings are for effective instruction. Effective instruction for beginning and problem readers teaches them to be aware of speech sounds (phonemes) and how they are represented in the writing system

Teachers and individual schools have the huge, vital task of finding the most effective method of teaching the children for whom they are responsible.
David Hamilton, 2002

(i.e. spelling–sound rules, syllable patterns) and of the meaningful units (morphemes) and their spelling patterns. These ideas lay the foundation of what teacher trainees need to be able to do. They should be at the heart of a curriculum for learning how to teach reading.

A core curriculum for learning how to teach reading

Specifically, a core curriculum for teacher preparation must include components for:

- understanding reading psychology and development;
- understanding the structure of the English language;
- applying best practices in all aspects of reading instruction;
- using validated, reliable, efficient assessments to inform classroom teaching.

This core curriculum can serve as the basis for inservice professional development for current teachers, many of whom have little awareness of the research-based knowledge on the reading process. In the United States the government has insisted that funding be provided only if the professional development is based on 'reliable, replicable research'. This funding proviso is intended to stop the development of programmes that are based on opinion and ideology rather than on scientific research.

Greater knowledge of phonics and phonemic awareness

In his submission to the Education and Science Select Committee, Professor Warwick Elley noted that New Zealand educators have developed a distinctive combination of strategies that work well with most pupils when properly applied. These methods include: language experience, shared reading, shared writing, lots of good books in the classroom, daily story reading by the teacher, time to conduct running records on each child, daily sessions of silent reading at class and at home, and guided silent reading under the teacher's supervision.

Yet the New Zealand approach to reading can be improved by the inclusion of phonics. An example comes from the study of children's reading development in the Manawatu, conducted by Tunmer and colleagues.[14] The teachers were taught to use a 'metacognitive' approach that was neither whole language nor skill and drill. Additional materials were introduced into the programmes of the new entrant classrooms. The materials were aimed at teaching **phonemic awareness** skills, knowledge of familiar **phonogram patterns**, the **sounds of the letters of the alphabet**, and some **simple word reading and spelling skills of phonics**. The results showed that children who received the modified instruction were significantly better in reading, and in attitudes to reading, than a similar group of children of the same age who had been assessed with the same set of reading measures in an earlier part of the study in 1993 but who had not received the modified teaching programme.

Teachers' need for better training to carry out systematic instruction in reading, spelling and writing should prompt action rather than criticism. It should highlight the existing gap between what teachers need and what they have been given. It should give weight to the obligation of teacher training programmes to provide candidates with a rigorous, research-based curriculum and opportunities to practise a range of predefined skills and knowledge. It should also emphasise the need for authorities to assess that knowledge.

All except 5 per cent of children can be taught to read. They deserve no less from their teachers. Teachers in turn deserve no less than the knowledge, skills and supported practice that will enable them to succeed in their teaching.

The American Federation of Teachers has put its weight behind more teaching of phonemic awareness and phonics. In *Teaching reading **is** rocket science*, published by the American Federation of Teachers, Moats[15] argues that teacher preparation must rest on a scientific foundation of solid research. Well-designed research has consistently supported these components and practices in reading instruction:

1. direct teaching of phonemic awareness;
2. systematic and explicit instruction in the code system of written English;
3. vocabulary instruction;
4. comprehension strategies;
5. opportunities to read on a daily basis.

Classroom instruction is crucial in preventing reading problems and it is a primary focus for effecting change. To improve classroom instruction, a comprehensive design of teacher preparation in reading instruction that defines the knowledge and skills necessary for effective practice is vital.

The vital role of individual teachers and schools

Furthermore, the weight of responsibility for the choice of method used in New Zealand schools lies with each individual school. In its submission to the Select Committee, the Ministry of Education put it this way:

> [D]ecisions about how to teach are made at the school level – that is, teaching methods are not prescribed as part of the national curriculum, although official guidance is provided through teacher handbooks and classroom learning materials.

The Ministry's teacher handbooks, such as *The learner as reader*, have a strong influence on how teachers apply this responsibility. Indeed, an illuminating footnote to the Ministry submission states that *The learner as reader* 'is currently being revised, on the recommendation of the Taskforce to provide more explicit guidance to meet the needs of struggling readers'. The statement speaks for itself.

The Ministry of Education likes to use the above opt-out clause that it does not force schools to teach reading in any one way. Yet its vast array of teacher resource materials, and all the reading materials produced for schools, send strong signals to teachers about what is required. Teacher training institutions take their direction from these documents, which are required reading for trainee teachers. The Ministry can't have it both ways: either it is accountable for what is taught in schools, or it is not accountable. If it is not accountable, it should not be sending out these signals about how to teach reading and should get out of the business of producing literacy materials and teacher resources for schools.

The responsibility resting on schools is reinforced by the Literacy Taskforce's recommendation that schools should be free to make their own decisions about how to teach reading. It stated that:

> ... decisions made about teaching strategies, teaching approaches, and materials to use are professional decisions that are best made at the local school level in response to the needs of particular groups of children and individuals.

Teachers and individual schools, therefore, have the huge, vital task of finding the most effective method of teaching the children for whom they are responsible. In this context, teacher training takes on even greater importance because, without thorough training in how children read and the theoretical background to this study, how can teachers possibly fulfil this role effectively? Without this knowledge, they are like the blind teaching the blind. To date they have not been equipped properly for this crucial task.

Development of knowledge of the language essentials

In the United States, Louisa Moats[16] surveyed hundreds of teachers about their theoretical orientation towards reading. She found that fewer than 5 to 10 per cent were able to name theorists or researchers whose work had influenced the teaching of reading.

To assess understanding of the English language, Moats[17] also gave a quiz (see appendix 2) to a group of 89 experienced teachers, including reading teachers, classroom teachers, speech language teachers, teaching assistants and graduate students who had enrolled in a course on reading, spelling and phonology. In their responses, even teachers who were literate and experienced generally showed that their grasp of spoken and written language structure was insufficient for them to be able to teach it explicitly to either beginning readers or those with reading/spelling difficulties. Teachers were unaware of the differences among phonetics, phonology and phonics and, although they had heard of phonological awareness, many were unsure of the number of phonemes in particular words. Many were unsure of what *speech sound* or *phoneme* meant. Knowledge of phonics was surprisingly weak.

In a similar study by Tom Nicholson in New Zealand,[18] a class of 83 teacher trainees were quizzed on their language knowledge, then were given lectures on language, and finally were quizzed again to see what they had learned. Like the results found by Moats, at the start of the course only 27 per cent of the class could consistently identify morphemes, only 10 per cent could identify consonant blends and none could identify digraphs. Less than half the class could count the phonemes in words and only 30 per cent knew the spelling rules that Moats had also tested. The best result was for counting syllables, completed successfully by 77 per cent of teachers. After the lectures, their test performance was much improved. The only exception was in the area of phonemes; only half the students understood the notion of a phoneme.

In terms of instructional implications, the message from the Moats and Nicholson studies is:

- even a few hours of lectures to teacher trainees can lead to considerable gains in knowledge of language, which is the basis for teaching phonics;
- some language essentials are harder to learn than others. Even experienced teachers may need additional instruction to gain a complete understanding of phonemic awareness, especially in regard to counting phonemes.

The problem can be tackled by making fundamental changes to the education system and to teacher training.

David Hamilton, 2002

Barriers to effecting change

In general, New Zealand teacher education is still in the hands of the established state providers: colleges of education, universities and polytechnics. As Geoffrey Partington wrote in his study for the Education Forum, it is hardly surprising that established providers can offer numerous testimonials of client satisfaction given that 'the same set of educational ideas is broadly shared by all key players in contemporary New Zealand education, apart from parents'.[19]

In preparing his report, Partington gained the impression that students had little opportunity to consider phonics methods as part of the range of strategies needed to teach reading. 'Instead', he observed, 'they are usually given a distorted "strawman" idea of what critics of whole language methods of learning to read wish to put in its place.' He found that young teachers graduating from the Christchurch College of Education said that its reading methods were uniformly hostile to phonetic methods. His concern was that teacher trainees are left unaware of phonics-based approaches or are at best given a brief and inadequate version of them, passing on a bias that has damaging effects.

When the whole language approach was first introduced, many of its inherent problems were not reflected in literacy levels in New Zealand schools, especially during the 1970s and early 1980s, because many educators and teacher trainees at this time still had some grounding in phonological awareness and were able to apply it informally. But the results of the Moats and Nicholson studies show clear language weaknesses among many trainee teachers and even experienced teachers nowadays.

There will continue to be huge resistance to any major changes in teacher training in the teaching of reading. For example, in one submission to the Select Committee, two lecturers from the Christchurch College of Education recommended that:

> It is important that no radical changes are made to the current methods of teaching reading in New Zealand school
>
> What has been proven is that a range of strategies should be employed. Teachers need up-skilling in these
>
> The emphasis should be on providing increased professional support for teachers so they can teach reading better. This will necessitate an increase in the availability of trained consultants, advisors etc.

There's gotta be a better way: my solutions

I propose that we tackle the problem by making fundamental changes at two levels: the education system itself and teacher training. Only with major reforms at both these levels can we establish a system of reading instruction that will allow 95 per cent of New Zealand children to learn to read.

Part A: Systemic changes

To eliminate the insidious influence of whole language and to prevent it doing further damage to children, major changes must be made to the education system. We cannot trust the Ministry of

Education or colleges of education to put it right. Too many of the stakeholders are committed to whole language, regardless of the research evidence stacked against it.

Here are the changes to the system that I believe are necessary:

1. Set up an **Office for the Review of Reading Standards (ORRS)**, which would be independent of influence from the Ministry of Education and would give independent advice to the government. ORRS would work with the Education Review Office to identify teachers who lacked the skills needed to teach phonics effectively. ORRS would provide these teachers with opportunities to improve their skills through retraining. Teachers would have to meet specified phonics training standards.

   ORRS would be responsible for following the progress of 'at risk' children. It would provide them with access to resources and reading assistance to ensure that they were not left behind in reading at school. Parents would be able to contact ORRS freely for help for their children. ORRS would be responsible for new initiatives in helping children who fell behind, placing them in innovative schemes to improve their reading skills.

   ORRS would also make independent reports to the government on ways to improve reading standards, and would conduct research. The National Institute for Child Health and Development in the United States is a good example of an agency that gives independent advice and conducts research designed to improve reading standards.

2. Provide **phonics training for Reading Recovery teachers and Resource Teachers of Literacy**. The Reading Recovery programme is not working well. It is 'more of the same' whole language approach, which itself is not working. It should be replaced by a strong phonological approach. Reading Recovery teachers need to be retrained to implement intensive phonics instruction for five- and six-year-old struggling readers.

   Resource Teachers of Literacy have responsibilities for teaching children with reading difficulties and advising teachers about reading. Yet they themselves lack skills in teaching phonics and should be required to undertake further training. Ironically, all Resource Teachers of Literacy are undergoing training through the Ministry of Education; however, the trainers are a consortium of colleges of education and other institutions that support whole language. Perhaps the proposed Office for the Review of Reading Standards could be influential in ensuring that the retraining gives reading teachers skills in teaching phonics.

3. Ensure **all teachers have phonics skills**. Teachers in mainstream classes do not have the skills to teach phonics effectively. They should be required to retrain or to take inservice courses taught

by phonics experts who can give them the phonics skills they need to teach reading effectively. The training could be outsourced to instructors with verifiable qualifications to train teachers in phonics instruction. The trainers themselves would need to engage in advanced training to ensure they were well qualified.

4. Provide **decodable graded readers that children can read** to replace the *Ready to Read* series. At the outset, children who are learning to use phonics must read books containing words that they can decode successfully. The present whole language series, *Ready to Read*, does not answer this need. Instead, it makes reading impossible for at least one child in four, forcing poor readers to guess and to rely on memory, rather than sound out words. The task of producing a new generation of graded, decodable readers could be outsourced to a company that has expertise in the production of excellent quality phonics books suitable for New Zealand children of today.

5. Produce a **phonics handbook for teachers** that explains the phonological approach to teaching reading. This text should replace the existing whole language teacher handbooks, *Reading in junior classes* and *The learner as reader*, which do not fit with recent research on reading. The new, comprehensive handbook would explain how to teach phonemic awareness and phonics in detail, and would provide practical illustrations and lesson plans, including CD-ROM and video support. The production of the text could be outsourced to a team of experts with qualifications in research and practice in the phonological approach.

6. Provide a **package of phonological literacy progress assessment of individual children that parents can understand**. It would give an accurate assessment of a child's reading skills on entry to school, especially phonemic awareness, and show reading and writing development through the grades. The assessment battery should use a wide range of measures, including norm-referenced tests that reliably assess progress through the first years of schooling to nine years of age. Through this package, parents would have access to reliable information about their children's reading and writing progress, and would be alerted immediately if there are problems.

   The assessment package for the younger children would include alphabet naming, phonemic awareness, non-word reading, word reading, reading of text, reading comprehension, spelling, writing of a story, and reading attitudes and habits. For children in later years, assessment packages would focus on more advanced reading and writing skills. The assessment measures should be researched by experts with knowledge of the assessment of children's phonological recoding skills especially in the early years.

Part B: Teacher training programmes

All trainee teachers should follow a programme of instruction that includes these courses:

1. **A course on phonological language fundamentals for teaching reading** would cover the crucial aspects of language needed for phonics, such as phonological awareness, morphemes, syllables, the history of the English language, and reading and spelling patterns.

2. **A course on teaching phonics** would cover the essentials of teaching phonics, beginning with the letter–sound rules of Anglo-Saxon words and proceeding to the more advanced rules of words of Latin, French and Greek origin. The course would include extensive practice in whole-class and small-group teaching of phonics.

3. **A course on the psychology and teaching of reading** would give teachers honest and fair coverage of the scientific literature on the reading process so that they gained a full understanding of how children learn to read and write, based on reliable, replicable research.

4. **A course on learning and reading disabilities** would involve teachers in 30 to 40 hours of practical tutoring of at least two children with reading difficulties, to give them professional skills in helping the child who has been left behind.

5. **A course on teaching reading comprehension** would show teachers how to improve comprehension of text by focusing on the improvement of vocabulary and strategies for analysing the structure of narrative and transactional (non-fiction) texts. This approach is important for all children, but especially for new immigrant children who are often strong in decoding skills but weak in their knowledge of English.

6. **A course on children's literature** would inform teachers about the best children's authors and those authors who write decodable books that beginning readers can enjoy (e.g. Dr Seuss). The ultimate goal of teaching phonics is to give children the skills to work out words independently so that they have access to the world of books.

A final word

New Zealand has the largest gap between good and bad readers in the OECD. One in four of our children are in remedial reading classrooms when they are only six years of age. Fifty per cent of our adults are unable to function effectively in literacy. Our schools teach with a reading method that has been denounced all over the world. Yet nothing is being done to throw out this failed approach and, as a consequence, thousands of children continue to suffer every year.

New Zealand wants to be a nation of readers. That is what we used to be, before the Ministry of Education committed us to the failed experiment of whole language. Too many children are missing out. What do they learn in school? They learn to hate reading and they learn that they are losers because they can't read. Is this what we want? If we want this country to be successful, rich and happy, then our children must be literate. A nation of literate children today is the key to our future and the present method of whole language is definitely not helping us to achieve this goal, so we must not be afraid to make the hard decisions. We must change our approach to reading instruction and move on. What sort of country are we to linger on and do nothing, even when we know what is right? We will look back one day in shame.

Notes

1 Nicholson, T. (1997). From ABC to Ready to Read. *Set: Research Information for Teachers*. Wellington: New Zealand Council for Educational Research.
See also: Nicholson, T. (2000). *Reading the writing on the wall: Debates, challenges and opportunities in the teaching of reading*. Palmerton North: Dunmore Press.

2 Ministry of Education. (1994). *English in the New Zealand school curriculum*. Wellington: Learning Media; p. 77.

3 Greaney, K.T. (2001). An investigation of teacher preferences for word identification strategies. *Australian Journal of Language and Literacy*, *24*, 23–30.

4 Hughes, K. (1999). *A survey of year 1–3 Auckland teachers' beliefs, approaches and practices in teaching reading*. Unpublished Master's thesis, University of Auckland, Auckland.

5 Nicholson, T., & Lam, R. (1998). Whole language teachers and phonics: Not 'do they' but 'how much is enough'? *Set: Research Information for Teachers*, *2*, article 6. Wellington: New Zealand Council for Educational Research.

6 Tunmer, W.E., Chapman, J.W., Ryan, H., & Prochnow, J. (1998). The importance of providing beginning readers with explicit training in phonological recoding skills. *Australian Journal of Learning Disabilities*, *3*, 4–14.

7 Castle, J., Riach, J., & Nicholson, T. (1994). Getting off to a better start in learning to read and spell: The effects of phonemic awareness instruction within a whole language programme. *Journal of Educational Psychology*, *86*, 350–359.

8 Ministry of Education. (1999). *Report of the Literacy Taskforce*. Wellington: Author.

9 Ministry of Education. (1999). *Report of the Literacy Experts Group to the Secretary of Education*. Wellington: Author.

10 Cited in Nicholson (2000) – see note 1.

11 Rath, L.K. (1995). *The phonemic awareness of reading teachers: Examining aspects of knowledge*. Unpublished doctoral dissertation, Harvard University, Boston.

12 Yopp, H.K. (1988). The validity and reliability of phonemic awareness tests. *Reading Research Quarterly*, *23*, 159–177.

13 Nicholson, T. (1999). *At the cutting edge: Recent research on learning to read and spell for success*. Wellington: New Zealand Council for Educational Research.

14 Tunmer, W.E., Chapman, J.W., Ryan, H., & Prochnow, J.E. (1998). The importance of providing beginning readers with explicit training in phonological processing skills. *Australian Journal of Learning Disabilities*, *3*, 4–14.

15 Moats, L.C. (1999). *Teaching reading* ***is*** *rocket science: What expert teachers of reading should know and be able to do*. [Online] American Federation of Teachers <www.aft.org/edissues/downloads/rocketsci.pdf>, accessed 30 May 2002.

16 Moats (1999) – see note 15.

17 Moats, L.C. (1995). The missing foundation in teacher education. *American Educator*, *19*, 9, 43–52.

18 Nicholson (1999) – see note 13.

19 Partington, G. (1997). *Teacher education and training in New Zealand*. Wellington: New Zealand Education Forum; p. 22.

APPENDIX 1

How to Teach Phonics – the Most Common Rules

The chart below represents the most regular letter–phoneme relationships. The information may be applied to any reading programme and provides enough word work for years one and two.

In the top half of the chart are all the consonant sounds to be learned; in the bottom half are all the vowel sounds. The strategy is to start with the simplest correspondences and work through to the more difficult. Work from left to right, starting with the 21 consonant single-letter sounds. Once children know the sounds of about half of the consonants, they can learn the short vowel sounds. Once they know one or two short sounds, they can begin to make two- and three-letter words. Once they learn some consonant clusters and consonant digraphs, they will read four-letter words. (See chapter 3 for more information.)

Regular letter–phoneme relationships

Consonants

Consonant single sounds	Consonant blends		Consonant digraphs	
	initial	**final**	**initial**	**final**
p g d b c	bl br cl cr dr	-ft -mp -nt -lk	ch sh th wh gh	-ng -ck -sh
y w l r t	fl fr gl gr sl			
f j m n w	pr tr sc sk scrt			
h k q x y z	spl sm squ sn str			
	sp st sw tw thr			

Vowels

Single vowel short	Single vowel long	*r* and *l* controlled vowels		Vowel digraphs	
		***r*-affected**	***l*-affected**	**one sound**	**two sounds**
a: made–made	o: hop–hope	ar: park	al: ball	ai–ay: rain–play	ea: beach–head
e: pet–Pete	u: cut–cute	or: for		ee: meet	ei: ceiling–eight
i: Tim–time		er: her		ie: piece	oo: moon–book
		ir: bird		oi–oy: oil–boy	ou: house–soup
		ur: fur		oa: boat	ow: cow–tow
				au–aw: sauce–law	
				ew: few	

Source: *Calfee, R.C., & Patrick, C.P. (1995).* Teach our children well. *Stanford, CA: Stanford University Alumni Association; p. 108. Reprinted with permission.*

Phonogram patterns

Teaching children to read three- and four-letter words can be made easier by using common spelling patterns and then changing just the beginning sounds. In this way it is possible to generate many words that follow the same pattern. In one study, Wylie and Durrell found that by using 37 phonogram patterns it was possible to generate over 500 different primary school level words.

Start with easy patterns like *–at* as in *cat, hat, mat, sat*. Later move to more difficult patterns like *–ight* as in *light, tight, fight, right*. The chart below lists the phonogram patterns that Wylie and Durrell used.

Sample of phonogram patterns

-ack	-ail	-ain	-ake	-ale	-ame	-an
-ank	-ap	-ash	-at	-ate	-aw	-ay
-eat	-ell	-est	-ice	-ick	-ide	-ight
-ill	-in	-ine	-ing	-ink	-ip	-ir
-ock	-oke	-op	-ore	-or		
-uck	-ug	-ump	-unk			

Source: *Wylie, R.E., & Durrell, D.D. (1970). Teaching vowels through phonograms.* Elementary English, 47, 787–791.

APPENDIX 2

Language Skills Quiz

Two studies[1] provided teachers and trainee teachers with the following language tasks (see chapter 7 for further details). Answers are given in italics.

1. From the list below, find an example of each of the following:

   scarecrow, nameless, terrible, phonograph, impeached, tables, weakly

   inflected verb ______________ *(impeached)*

   compound noun ______________ *(scarecrow)*

   bound root ______________ *(phonograph)*

   derivational suffix ______________ *(nameless)*

2. For each word on the left, determine the number of syllables and the number of morphemes:

	Syllables	Morphemes
salamander	*4*	*1*
crocodile	*3*	*1*
attached	*2*	*3*
unbelievable	*5*	*3*
finger	*2*	*1*
pies	*1*	*2*
gardener	*3*	*2*
psychometrics	*4*	*3*

3. How many speech sounds are in the following words?

ox	*3*	boil	*3*
king	*3*	thank	*4*
straight	*5*	shout	*3*
though	*2*	precious	*6*

4. What is the third speech sound in each of the following words?

boyfriend	/f/	prayer	/e/
thankyou	/ŋ/	higher	/r/ or /y/
squabble	/w/	chalk	/k/
educate	/y/ or /yu/	stood	/ʊ/

5. Underline the schwa vowels:
   about melody sofa effect difficult definition

6. Underline the consonant blends:
   doubt known first pumpkin squawk scratch

7. Underline the consonant digraphs:
   wholesale psychic doubt wrap daughter think

8. When is a 'ck' used in spelling?
   (immediately after a short, stressed vowel)

9. What letters signal that a 'g' is pronounced ? *(e, i, y)*

10. List all the ways you can think of to spell /k/: ***(c, k, ck, ch)***

    Note: qu and x also correspond to /kw/ and /ks/

11. What are six common syllable types in English?
    (Open, closed, r-controlled, vowel team, silent -e, consonant -le)

12. When adding a suffix to a word ending with 'y', what is the rule?
    (When a root word ends in a ***y*** *preceded by a consonant, change* ***y*** *to* ***i*** *when adding a suffix, except if the suffix is* ***-ing****. If the root word ends in a* ***y*** *preceded by a vowel, just add the suffix.)*

13. How can you recognise a word of Greek origin?
    (Presence of ***y*** *for /i/ as in* ***gym****;* ***ch*** *for /k/ as in* ***chorus****;* ***ph*** *of /f/ as in* ***sphere****; or a Greek combining form such as* ***psych+ology****)*

14. Account for the double 'm' in comment or commitment.
    (The first ***m*** *closes the syllable to make it short;* ***com*** *is a Latin morpheme, as are* ***ment*** *and* ***mit****.)*

Note

1 Moats, L.C. (1995). The missing foundation in teacher education. American Educator, 19, 9, 43–52.
Nicholson, T. (1999). *At the cutting edge: Recent research on learning to read and spell for success.* Wellington: New Zealand Council for Educational Research.